Norman S. Newton

Kintyre

Pevensey Island Guides

Thanks to Sue Fortune and the staff of
Campbeltown Public Library; to the
staff of the Tourist Information Centre
in Campbeltown; to John Carmichael of
the Campbeltown Heritage Centre; to
Frances Hood and Angus Martin, for
useful advice and information; to
A. I. B. Stewart, for his inspiration; to
the late Lachie MacKinnon, for his
commitment to tourism in Kintyre; to
the photographer, Derek Croucher, for
his sympathetic eye and professional
skill; and to the staff of David & Charles,
the publishers, for their constant
support and encouragement.

The Pevensey Press is an imprint of
David & Charles

First published in the UK in 1999

Text Copyright © Norman Newton 1999
Photography Copyright © Derek Croucher
1998
Layout Copyright © David & Charles 1999

A catalogue record for this book is available
from the British Library.

ISBN 1 898630 01 1

Printed in Hong Kong by
Wing King Tong Ltd
for David & Charles
Brunel House   Newton Abbot   Devon

CONTENTS

Pages 1 & 2–3: Tarbert harbour

Left: Sunset over West Loch Tarbert and Islay from near Whitehouse

Overleaf: Looking across Kilbrannan Sound to Arran, from Escart Farm

INTRODUCING KINTYRE

THE LONG, NARROW peninsula of Kintyre points like an aged, gnarled finger from the Gaelic heartland of Scotland, Argyll, southwards to the Gaelic homeland, the Antrim coasts and glens in Northern Ireland. The peninsula is about 40 miles (64km) from north to south, and 6–8 miles (9.7–12.9km) in width, with Atlantic rollers crashing into its western coastline, and the more sheltered waters of the Firth of Clyde to the east. Just off the west coast of Kintyre is the little island of Gigha, and beyond that are the islands of the southern Hebrides, Islay and Jura. To the east of Kintyre is the mountainous island of Arran, on the other side of the Kilbrannan Sound, 3 miles (4.8km) across at its narrowest.

So, from the Mull of Kintyre, the headland at the south end of the peninsula, popularised by Paul McCartney's hit single of 1977, the view is of the coastline of Antrim, and the L-shaped island of Rathlin, which featured in Scottish history as one of the hiding places of Robert the Bruce, Scotland's hero-king who fought the English at Bannockburn, in 1314, and inflicted a crushing defeat on the 'Auld Enemy'.

Above: Skipness Chapel with the Isle of Arran beyond

Opposite: Coastal scenery north of the Mull of Kintyre

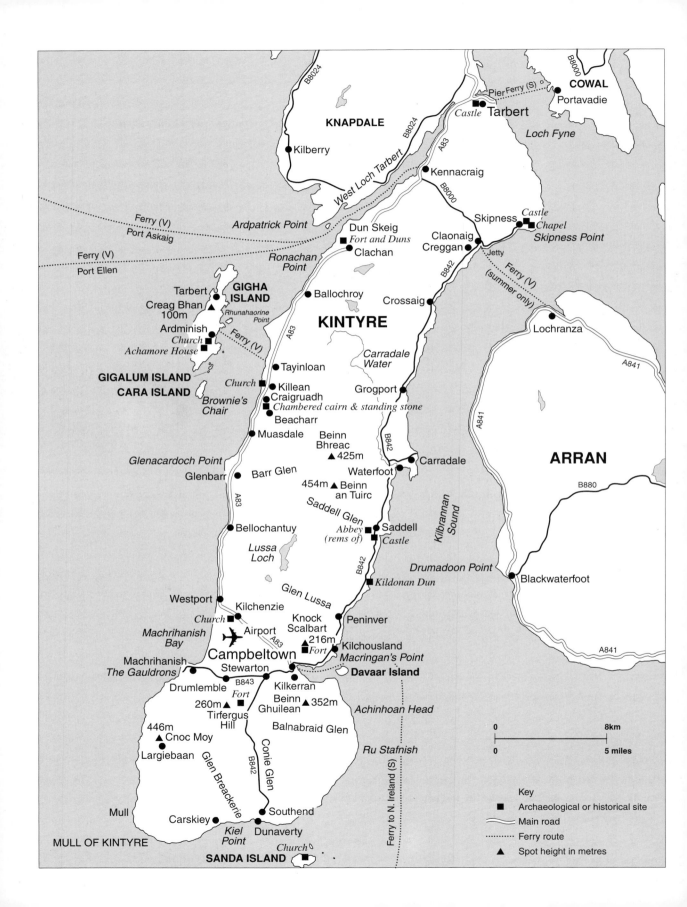

But in earlier centuries it was not the English who were the main threat to the Gaelic-speaking Scots of Argyll, but the Norse adventurers, pillagers and eventually peaceful settlers whom we know as Vikings. And it was King Magnus of Norway who headed several marauding expeditions to the Hebrides in the 1090s, and defined the northern extent of Kintyre.

The Norse had moved into the Hebrides in the early 800s, and had established a base on the Isle of Man. They had had their eye on Kintyre for some time, and many even settled there, their Norse farm names and landscape names surviving even to the present: Carradale, Saddell, Skipness, Muasdale and Ormsary, and many other examples, were named by the Norse incomers. But in 1098, Magnus concluded a treaty with the King of the Scots, formalising the Norse territorial claim to the Western Isles, all occupied and administered by Scandinavian rulers to a greater or lesser extent for 300 years.

The political will to conclude a settlement between the rulers of Scotland and Norway was handed over to the lawyers to sort out, and they agreed a form of words which would effectively allow Magnus to keep all the islands that he claimed through right of occupation – 'all the islands off the west coast which were separated by water navigable by a ship with the rudder set' – according to the *Orkneyinga Saga*. Magnus adopted local dress while on his Hebridean expeditions, wearing the knee-length tunic still seen on medieval West Highland gravestones, and gained the nickname Magnus 'Barelegs'. Now he used local knowledge to lay claim to the Kintyre peninsula. The isthmus at Tarbert, at the north end of the peninsula, narrows to only 1600 yards (1460m) and it was common practice for the locals to move their little fishing skiffs across this narrow neck of land from one sea loch to another. Magnus sat in one such skiff, held the tiller firmly, and was pulled across the isthmus on rollers, from east to west. The Norse chronicler was triumphant. Kintyre (the Norse called it *Satiri*) was, he said, 'more valuable than the best of all the Hebridean islands' – though, he added in fairness, 'not as good as the Isle of Man'.

Most of the landscape of Kintyre consists of a ridge of low hills running down the middle of the peninsula, with small river valleys and a few larger glens dissecting the landscape. However, near the southern end of the peninsula a geological fault line interrupts this pattern, and the hills terminate abruptly, overlooking a triangular plain of low-lying, fertile ground known as the Laggan. On the west side of the Laggan are 6 miles (9·7km) of sandy beach backed by sand dunes, with the village and golf course of Machrihanish at its southern end. On the east side of the Laggan is Campbeltown Loch, with the town of Campbeltown at its head.

The main road from Tarbert to Campbeltown runs down the west side of the peninsula, keeping to the raised beach for most of its length before turning eastwards across the Laggan to its final destination. On the way, the road passes through the villages of Clachan, Tayinloan, Glenbarr, Muasdale, Bellochantuy and Kilkenzie. An alternative route to Campbeltown crosses

CANTYRE

Kintyre was still described as 'Cantyre' well into the nineteenth century – a spelling which more closely resembles the original Gaelic name of the peninsula, ceann tire, the 'head of the land', the Land's End of Argyll – earr a' Ghaidheal, 'the land of the Gaels'. Kintyre is very likely the first part of Scotland where the Gaelic language was spoken. Gaelic was the mother tongue of a tribal people who invaded or occupied Kintyre and other areas of south-west Scotland in what historians used to call the Dark Ages, meaning the period after the collapse of the Roman Empire when the political organisation of the British Isles was redefined and reorganised, from roughly AD400–AD600. It was a period of change and complexity, but the academics think that they have now shed enough light on the gloomier recesses of this barely documented period of our history to call it the Early Historic Period.

The departing Romans had given Latin names to all the tribes and peoples with whom they came into contact, and their name for the people of the island we call Ireland was the Scotti. *It was some of these* Scotti *who moved across the 12 miles (19km) of the North Channel from Antrim to Kintyre, bringing their language and culture with them. In Argyll they established what came to be known as the Kingdom of Dalriada (Dal-riata, the portion of the tribe from the 'Root', the Glens of Antrim).*

Fishing for mackerel off the pier at Campbeltown

over to the east side of the peninsula just south of Tarbert, reaching the Kilbrannan Sound at Skipness, with its superb medieval castle and chapel, then runs down the east side of Kintyre, through Grogport, Carradale, Saddell and Peninver to 'The Wee Toon', as Campbeltown is affectionately known to its natives.

Before 1609, it was known to its then Gaelic-speaking natives as *Ceann loch cille Chiaran*, 'the head of the loch of Ciaran', the local saint. In the political chaos which afflicted Argyll after the crushing and forfeiture of the powerful local magnates, the MacDonald Lords of the Isles, the Campbell clan were authorised by the Scottish Crown to bring stability and security to Kintyre and with characteristic Campbell modesty they named the principal town, with its royal castle, after themselves.

South of Campbeltown, the main road leads down the middle of the peninsula, turning off the Campbeltown to Machrihanish road at Stewarton. Between Stewarton and Machrihanish is the old mining village of Drumlemble. From the Stewarton turn-off it is an easy run of a little over 8 miles (13km) to Southend, scene of the infamous massacre at Dunaverty castle in 1647. Offshore is the occasionally inhabited island of Sanda.

Left: View of Campbeltown, nestling at the head of Campbeltown Loch

POPULATION

There are two towns in Kintyre: Tarbert (Gaelic tair-beart, a place over which a boat can be drawn, a portage) is situated on the isthmus at the north edge of the peninsula, with a population of 1,347; Campbeltown, on its Loch, is the administrative centre of the peninsula, with 5,600 inhabitants (1991 Census). One distillery remains where once there were over 30, fortunately still producing single-malt whisky of excellent quality, and a handful of fishing boats preserve another traditional industry, where once the harbour was packed from side to side with the ring-net fleet. A handful of light industries, including a cheese factory and fish-processing plants, keep Campbeltown from economic disaster. The tourist industry, along with farming and forestry, keeps the economy of Kintyre reasonably buoyant.

The other settlements in Kintyre are tiny villages, spread out around the coast, often sitting on 'raised beaches'. These are geological features dating from the end of the last Ice Age and reflect changes in sea level which only finally settled down in this part of Scotland around 6,000BC. The population of the whole peninsula, including Campbeltown and Tarbert, was 10,957 at the 1991 Census.

An alternative route to Southend from Campbeltown is the scenic but demanding 'Leerside' (leewardside) road. Running along the south shore of Campbeltown Loch, it passes the Doirlinn, which as its Gaelic name suggests is a dog-legged gravel and shingle feature, never more than a few yards wide, which connects the mainland to Davaar Island at low tide. As the Doirlinn is covered at high tide, and floods alarmingly rapidly, visitors intending to cross over to Davaar Island to view the famous Crucifixion cave painting there are advised to check locally for tide times. They are published in the local paper and posted at the Tourist Information Centre in Campbeltown, at the pier.

From Southend, a single-track road climbs up from the shore to cross high, desolate moorland, heading west for the Mull of Kintyre lighthouse. Eight miles (13km) of steep, twisting, tortuous road – in places barely more than a track – end in a car park overlooking the lighthouse. The views are spectacular – to Ireland, Rathlin Island, Islay and Jura.

After this initial whirlwind tour of Kintyre, it is time to consider some practicalities. Getting there is easy enough, with a range of options available. A daily flight from Glasgow Airport lands at Machrihanish airfield,

Right: Carradale Bay from Carradale golf course

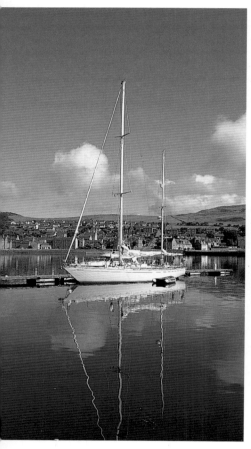

Campbeltown harbour

Opposite: The car ferry which links Campbeltown and Ballycastle in Northern Ireland

formerly a massive RAF airbase, with reputedly one of the longest runways in the world. The base was also home to the SEALS, a US Navy special forces unit. The withdrawal and closure of these facilities was a severe blow to the local economy. The little civilian aircraft landing at Machrihanish are dwarfed by the military surroundings.

Most visitors to Campbeltown arrive by road. The bus from Glasgow takes 4¹⁄₂ hours, and car drivers new to Argyll roads will need to allow well over 3 hours for the 135 mile (217km) journey, depending on local conditions. The main road has been greatly improved in recent years, but the coastal road down the east side of Kintyre, though scenically beautiful, is slow going.

In the summer months, a car ferry links Campbeltown to the port of Ballycastle, in Northern Ireland; a smaller car ferry sails from the village of Claonaig (near Skipness) to Lochranza, at the north end of the Isle of Arran.

All year round a car ferry connects Gigha to Kintyre at Tayinloan, while a large car ferry sails daily from Kennacraig (West Loch Tarbert) to Islay.

However, there is no disguising the fact that basically Kintyre is a *cul-de-sac*, at the extremity of the road network in what is already a wild and isolated part of the country. That so many visitors make this journey not just once, but over and over again, over many years, suggests that Kintyre has something special to offer.

Many of its attractions are linked to outdoor pursuits, so adequate raingear and footwear are essential. The wind and rain can be awesome, but in the tourist season bad weather does not generally last long – the gales blow it away in a day or two at most, and sometimes within the hour! Kintyre is not a place for mountaineers, but the walking is unrivalled, and there are excellent local guidebooks.

There are particular aspects to Kintyre which attract specialists from far and wide. The geology is varied and fascinating. The archaeology and ancient history of Kintyre are represented by burial cairns, standing stones and various types of Iron Age forts, many of them better preserved than is normally the case in our over-cultivated and over-developed environment. There are ruined medieval castles at Tarbert, Skipness and Dunaverty, and medieval chapels all over the peninsula.

The bird life of Kintyre attracts its own inimitable breed of 'twitchers', while the mild Atlantic climate, despite apparently incessant wind and rain in the winter months, creates an unusual range of habitats – palm trees grow in Campbeltown gardens and along the seafront, when unmolested by vandals. The shoreline is interesting, especially to children, with a good number of safe, sandy beaches, and also superb surfing conditions for those interested in living more dangerously.

Maggie's Cottage, An Tairbeart Heritage Centre

Opposite: Dun Skeig hill fort and West Loch Tarbert

In recent years Kintyre has even started to provide wet weather attractions for its visitors, with community museums and 'heritage centres' springing up all over the place. Some will no doubt prove ephemeral, but others are a notable asset to the local communities and the local economy. The An Tairbeart Heritage Centre (at Tarbert) leads the way in this new kind of tourism, while Campbeltown Museum, though little changed in a hundred years, exhibits archaeological material of national importance, such as the famous jet necklace from the burial cairn at Beacharr. Campbeltown Public Library, which shares a lovely little sandstone building with the Museum, has an excellent local history collection.

In this book we will explore all of the reasonably accessible parts of Kintyre, with suggestions for more adventurous wanderings by more intrepid visitors. A day excursion to the island of Gigha is something all visitors to Kintyre should include in their plans, and we will include that little gem of an island in our meanderings. Kintyre's history is exciting, sometimes tragic, and often violent, so we will include enough historical material to render the past and its relics understandable, and leave readers interested in the minutiae of clan history to explore some of the suggestions for further reading in our booklist.

Kintyre's main asset, its prime visitor attraction, is its people, and we invite visitors to partake of local hospitality and to respond to the openness and friendliness that is so characteristic of Argyll. The coastal scenery may be magnificent, the archaeology very special indeed, and the wildlife rich and varied, but it is the friendly and unpretentious folk of Kintyre who make this peninsula – almost an island – so unforgettable.

1 THE GATEWAY TO KINTYRE – TARBERT

PPROACHING KINTYRE FROM the north, the main road from Glasgow heads south at Lochgilphead, running through Ardrishaig at the southern end of the Crinan Canal, then twisting round the eastern shores of Knapdale, past the former Campbell home at Stonefield, now an exclusive hotel, until suddenly reaching the little village of Tarbert, which guards the narrow isthmus and keeps the peninsula of Kintyre from being a true island. Often regarded as insular in the sociological sense, part of the charm of Kintyre is that it is relatively unspoilt, a wonderful part of Argyll which repays exploration.

With a resident population of around 1,300 (1991 Census), Tarbert has a little over 10 per cent of the population of Kintyre. Its industries are fishing and tourism, with a good variety of shops and services, including an excellent bookshop and a Tourist Information Centre (tel: 01880 820429). In the little harbour, local fishing boats and visiting yachts create an atmosphere of colour and activity. Out in the middle of the harbour is a square stone feature, an artificial island known as the Bielding, used to manoeuvre sailing vessels into the inner basin when the wind was contrary.

Above: Tarbert harbour attracts many visiting yachts

Opposite: Splashes of colour beautifully reflected in Tarbert harbour

The village was founded in the Middle Ages. It became a royal burgh in the closing years of the reign of Robert I, when Tarbert Castle was being enlarged and strengthened, between 1325 and 1329. Its real period of growth and prosperity came in the first half of the nineteenth century with the development of the fishing fleet, especially with the ring-net fishing for herring. Harbour improvements were made the 1820s under the direction of Thomas Telford, though plans to build a canal across the isthmus never reached fruition.

On the north side of the harbour is a fine pontoon berthing area which can accommodate about 200 leisure craft. Tarbert has always been important to the Clyde yachting scene, and still has an active sailing club. Each May, it hosts the second largest racing programme in the UK, when around 300 boats and 3,000 people arrive in the village for the annual regatta. There are many hotels, guest houses and B & B houses to choose from for accommodation.

From the East Pier at Tarbert there is a ferry service to Cowal, to the former construction yard at Portavadie, where platforms for North Sea oil exploration were to be built. Sadly, the vastly expensive project failed. The road system through Cowal is inadequate for modern needs, but if you are not in a hurry the surrounding scenery makes it worth putting up with the inconvenience of single-track roads and the lack of tourist facilities. From Portavadie it is a short drive to Colintraive, where there is a ferry to the island of Bute – and the possibility of catching the car ferry at Rothesay across the Firth of Clyde to Wemyss Bay.

The houses and shops fronting the harbour date from the period of redevelopment in the early nineteenth century; the older part of the village lies up the hill, inland, though nothing now remains of medieval Tarbert. The earliest houses are in Castle Street, where a row of slated cottages dates from around 1800. The only building of distinction is the church, standing on the southern edge of the town, on the highest point of the road across the isthmus.

Tarbert was the setting for the novel *Gillespie*, by George MacDougall Hay (1881–1919). First published in 1914, it has since been reprinted (Canongate, 1979; paperback edition, 1983). In the introduction to the reprint edition, the main character, Gillespie Strang, is described as 'the agent of modernisation and capitalist enterprise in a basically peasant society'. Tirelessly scheming and tenacious, Gillespie is predatory, manipulative and full of malice – but is also seen by some in the story as a

Left: Tarbert harbour, popular with the Clyde yachting fraternity and (above) Tarbert church window

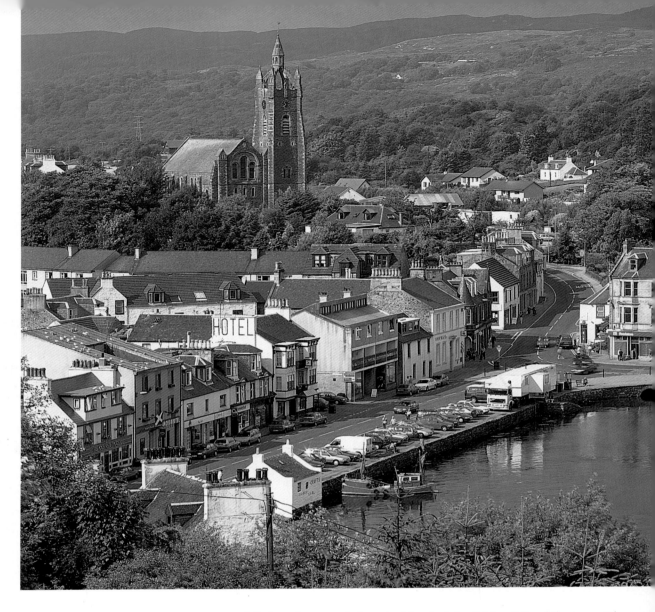

The view of Tarbert from the castle, with the church prominent

public benefactor and the true friend of the fishing folk of the town. The book is full of local colour and accurate historical and social detail, and has been compared with the works of Robert Louis Stevenson, George Douglas Brown (*The House with the Green Shutters*), James Hogg, and even Melville's *Moby Dick*. Hay was a Church of Scotland minister, a native of Tarbert, and set his novel in 'Brieston', a thinly disguised fictional version of his native town. His son George Campbell Hay (1915–1984) is regarded as one of Scotland's leading poets, writing in Gaelic and English.

TARBERT CASTLE

Overlooking the village of Tarbert is Tarbert Castle, its ruined tower dating from the 1490s. However, the real complexity of the site, and its age, is

The ruins of Tarbert castle, a royal fortress

revealed only when exploring the sometimes rather indistinct humps and bumps to the south-west of the castle tower, where can be found the square Inner Bailey, possibly the remains of a royal castle built in the middle of the thirteenth century, in the reign of Alexander II or Alexander III. The remains of the curtain wall which formed the Outer Bailey can just be traced around the perimeter of the rocky knoll on it stands.

Tarbert Castle was strengthened and renovated in the 1320s by Robert the Bruce, following the Wars of Independence, presumably to guard the western flanks of his kingdom against the threat of the MacDonald Lords of the Isles. Because it was a royal castle, a number of building accounts have survived in the Scottish Exchequer Rolls, in which three masons are named; the cost of rebuilding the walls, and other associated works, was £282 15 shillings.

Tarbert was visited by James IV in 1494 during his visit to Kintyre, and it was at this time that the tower house was constructed. No doubt additions and alterations continued over the decades, especially after it became a Campbell stronghold – it was granted to the Earl of Argyll in 1504. The castle is well worth a visit, and walkways and interpretative panels explain its complicated layout and history. The tower house itself is in a dangerous condition. A trust was set up in 1990 with the aim of developing and preserving this historic site.

AN TAIRBEART HERITAGE CENTRE

On the outskirts of Tarbert, on the main A83 road to Campbeltown, is the new Heritage Centre and Agricultural Museum of An Tairbeart (tel: 01880 820190), with a bookshop, excellent restaurant and a varied programme of events designed to interpret and explain traditional crafts and farming practices. The award-winning centre is set in 86 acres (35ha) of woodland, through which are guided walks, ending in fine viewpoints. There are Highland cattle, other native breeds including sheep and ponies, and a play area for children. A variety of habitats, including native woodland, bog, moorland and pasture gives a tremendous range of plant and bird life in a small area. The exhibition area in the heritage centre gives a good explanation of the ecology of a crofting township. There is an admission charge to the exhibition and grounds.

An Tairbeart Heritage Centre, Tarbert, exhibits the agricultural history of Kintyre. The pigs enjoying a sunny snooze are similar to those which would have been farmed in the Iron Age. The centre also offers lovely woodland walks

LEGEND OF KING MAGNUS

The legend of Magnus Barelegs and how he claimed Kintyre as a Norse 'island' by having his skiff dragged across the isthmus at Tarbert is a story well known locally. He seems to have made several expeditions to the Hebrides in the 1090s in an attempt to reassert Norse sovereignty over the area. Accounts of his exploits appear in several of the Norse sagas; in the *Orkneyinga Saga* there is a vivid account of his expedition of 1093:

> King Magnus was making his way north along the Scottish coast when messengers from King Malcolm of Scotland came to offer him a settlement: King Malcolm would let him have all the islands off the west coast which were separated by water navigable by a ship with the rudder set. When King Magnus reached Kintyre he had a skiff hauled across the narrow neck of land at Tarbert, with himself sitting at the helm, and this is how he won the whole peninsula. Kintyre is thought to be more valuable than the best of the Hebridean islands, though not as good as the Isle of Man. It juts out from the west of Scotland, and the isthmus connecting it to the mainland is so narrow that ships are regularly hauled across. From there, King Magnus sailed to the Hebrides and sent some of his men over to the Minch. They were to row close to the shore, some northwards, others south, and that is how he claimed all the islands west of Scotland.

This authoritative Norse account gives a hint that Magnus may have been in the Clyde, negotiating with Malcolm's emissaries, and this is confirmed from another source, Snorro Sturlason's *Magnus Saga*:

> King Magnus brought his ships up to the south of Satiri [Kintyre]. Then he had a small ship drawn across the ridge of Satiri, and the helm laid across in its proper form. The king himself sat down in the poop, and took hold of the helm-ball; and thus he got possession of all the country lying on the larboard side.

This extract indicates quite clearly that Magnus crossed the isthmus at Tarbert from east to west. The starboard side of a vessel takes its name from the steering oar which was on the right-hand side of a Viking long-ship.

Another extract from the *Magnus Saga* gives some idea of the importance of King Magnus in the Norse world, even allowing for inevitable exaggeration and flattery:

> King Magnus wore on his head a helmet, and carried on his arm a red shield, emblazoned with a golden lion; in his belt was a sword

THE ORKNEYINGA SAGA

The Orkneyinga Saga *is the history of the Earls of Orkney, written down in Iceland early in the thirteenth century, though parts of it are derived from earlier oral traditions. It covers events in Orkney, Caithness and the Hebrides from the ninth to the twelfth centuries. Written in a distinctively poetic and sometimes imaginative style, and intended to amplify the achievements of the main characters and to entertain its readers, it nevertheless is an important historical source.*

of exceeding sharpness, the hilt of which was ivory, enwreathed with inlaid gold; in his hand was a javelin; and over his coat of mail fell a short silken tunic of ruby colour, embroidered with a lion of auric hue; and all acknowledged that none could surpass him in dignity and beauty.

On the other hand, the *Heimskringla* gives some idea of just how much the local people had to fear from this royal visitor:

And when Magnus came to the Hebrides he began at once to plunder and burn the inhabited lands, and he slew the menfolk. And they robbed everything wherever they went. But the people of the land fled far and wide; some to Scotland's firths, some south to Kintyre, or over to Ireland. Some received quarter and did homage.

The branch-scorcher [fire] played greedily up into the sky in Lewis; there was far and wide an eager going in flight. Flame spouted from the houses. The active King ravaged Uist with fire. The King made red the sword of battle. The farmers lost life and wealth.

The diminisher of the battle-gosling's hunger caused Skye to be plundered; the glad wolf reddened tooth in many a mortal wound upon Tiree. The Scots-expeller went mightily; the people in Mull ran to exhaustion. Greenland's King caused maids to weep, south in the islands.

Wide bore the active King his shields upon the level sand island [Tiree]; there was smoke from Islay when the King's men stirred up the burning. The sons of men south in Kintyre bowed beneath the swords' edges. The valiant battle-quickener then planned the Manxmen's fall.

So, this was a campaign of terror and devastation, and when remembering the romantic picture of Magnus being dragged across the isthmus of Tarbert it is perhaps well to spare a thought for the associated mayhem and suffering he perpetrated on the men and women who got in his way.

HEIMSKRINGLA

Snorri's Sturluson's Heimskringla, 'The Circle of the Worlds', describes the viewpoint of a thirteenth-century chieftain, a lawyer, poet and patriot, looking back across two hundred years of history to the time when the kingdom of Norway was created. Although it is primarily concerned with extolling the achievements of King Olaf Haraldsson (Saint Olaf), there is much incidental detail shedding light on events in the Hebrides and Kintyre.

2 THE EAST SIDE

FROM TARBERT, THE MAIN A83 Campbeltown road heads south along West Loch Tarbert. The road now by-passes the old ferry pier, from where the *Lochiel* and her predecessors sailed for Islay and Jura. Today there is a new ferry terminal at Kennacraig,further down the loch, from where there are frequent sailings to Port Ellen and Port Askaig on Islay. On summer Wednesdays the service continues to Colonsay and Oban, allowing the luxury of a day-trip to Colonsay.

Just past the Kennacraig ferry terminal, about five miles south of Tarbert, the minor road with passing places, the B8001, strikes off to the east, heading over the ridge of Kintyre for the east coast villages of Claonaig and Skipness. Near the high point of this road the extravagant house on the road side is Spion Kop, named after a skirmish in the Boer War. As the road descends through Glenrisdell the landscape is transformed from bare moorland to the fertile pastures of the narrow coastal fringes of the sheltered east coast of Kintyre.

At Claonaig there is a ferry terminal connecting to Lochranza on the island of Arran – one of the joys of a holiday in Argyll is to explore the diversity of ferry connections and engage in some serious island-hopping. At present this service operates only in the summer months. Once in Arran, it is possible to continue across the Firth of Clyde using the ferry service from Brodick to Ardrossan, though advance booking is strongly recommended. Information on all ferry services is available from Caledonian MacBrayne's head office in Gourock (tel: 01475 650100).

Kilbrannan Sound and Arran from the road above Claonaig

SKIPNESS CASTLE

Past the Claonaig ferry slipway, continue for another two miles to Skipness, a tiny village with one of the most magnificent buildings in Argyll – Skipness Castle. Skipness also has one of the most curious little monuments in Argyll – the War Memorial, erected soon after 1918, has a clock incorporated into its design. Now in the care of Historic Scotland, Skipness Castle is open to the public and is well interpreted in display panels.

The ferry leaving Claonaig for Arran

Unfortunately there is no car parking at the castle so visitors are faced with a stroll of about ten minutes along what is effectively the entrance drive to Skipness House, a private residence.

Skipness Castle guards the northern entrance to Kilbrannan Sound, the seaway between Kintyre and Arran. It also looks across the Firth of Clyde to the Stewart lands in the kingdom of Scotland. Although this is one of the major medieval fortresses of the western seaboard, little is known of its early history. A document of 1261 records that it was then in the possession of Dugald MacSween, who presumably held it for the MacDonald Lords of the Isles. It is likely that the first castle on the site, with a chapel, was built in the first half of the thirteenth century. Traces of this first hall-house and its chapel can still be seen in the fabric of the surviving walls.

The castle was enlarged and strengthened in the early 1300s, and then, probably in the 1490s, the surviving south-east tower was added. Towards the end of the sixteenth century this tower was further added to and became a more domesticated tower house. After the forfeiture of the Lords of the Isles in 1493, Skipness Castle reverted to the Crown and was granted first to Sir Duncan Forestare, an officer in the royal household, and subsequently to Archibald, 2nd Earl of Argyll. It remained in the hands of various minor branches of the Campbell family until the middle of the nineteenth century. It was abandoned as a residence soon before 1700, and by 1800 had been converted into farm buildings and offices, which were removed in 1898 by the landowner, R. C. Graham, who then started the process of restoration which is still continuing.

Skipness was a 'castle of enceinte' relying for its defence on the strength of its tall, thick curtain walls. The once free-standing hall-house occupied what is now the north-west corner of the present courtyard; it is likely to have been a building of three storeys, with the ground floor used as a

The tower house of Skipness Castle dating from the 1490s

cellar, for storage, and the top two floors as the residence. The first floor windows of the hall-house can still be seen in the fabric of the curtain wall, and on the other side of the courtyard the windows of the early thirteenth century chapel, built at the same time as the hall-house, can also be seen. This early chapel was dedicated to St Columba.

The most impressive feature of Skipness Castle is the gatehouse, of two storeys, of which the upper contains a portcullis chamber. Some of its original splendour has been spoiled by the robbing of the dressed sandstone which is such a feature of the castle – probably brought across from quarries near Lochranza, in Arran. The whole impression is of medieval power and prestige, a massive fortress built in a primitive and remote area.

KILBRANNAN CHAPEL

Nearby is the equally impressive Kilbrannan Chapel, as poorly documented as the castle but thought to date from the late thirteenth or early fourteenth century. Details of its construction and architecture, especially the use of dressed sandstone, suggest that it was built by the same masons who enlarged the walls of Skipness Castle. This chapel was dedicated to St Brendan.

Dressed sandstone blocks from Arran in the chapel at Skipness

There are many interesting stones in the surrounding graveyard, including five recumbent tombstones in the distinctive late-medieval style found in several of Kintyre's other medieval chapels. These are now housed in protective boxes. Attached to the south wall of the chapel is the burial enclosure of the Campbells of Skipness, with decorative mural monuments. There are several eighteenth-century tombstones in the graveyard, including one with an illustration of a four-horse plough team, commemorating 'Angus Mckinnin in Sron' (Strone), who died in 1739. The stone for William Ferreor, gardener in Skipness, is dated 1727 and contains carved representations of garden tools.

CARRADALE

From Skipness and Claonaig a twisting, single-track road runs down the east coast of Kintyre to Carradale, passing a series of farms which give evidence of Norse occupation in their place-names: Oragaig, Crossaig, Sunadale. At the north end of this road both Claonaig and Skipness are Norse in origin, while Carradale is another Norse name. This coastal road is magnificently scenic, with views across Kilbrannan Sound to the jagged mountains of the north end of Arran. A feature of this road used to be the many hump-back bridges, but lately the approaches to most of them have been smoothed off to avoid modern tour buses grounding inelegantly.

From Claonaig to Carradale is about 15 miles (24km), but the twisty road means that this is not a journey to be made in a hurry. The shore at Grogport is a good place for a picnic: across the road is the remains of a prehistoric 'cist' (stone box) grave, known locally as 'The Sailor's Grave'. It is likely to be more than 4,000 years old. Neolithic cists occur all over Kintyre, but not many of them are so easy to visit!

Carradale has much to offer: a golf course, a castle, forest walks, a vitrified Iron Age hill fort, a safe, sandy beach, and a much-improved harbour, with its fishing fleet. Nearby is Carradale House, with its attractive gardens, the Argyll home of Naomi Mitchison, perhaps the most important Scottish female writer of the twentieth century. Carradale has been catering for the tourist trade for most of this century, and is a favourite holiday destination for Glaswegians. There is plenty of holiday accommodation, though, of course, it fills up quickly in the summer season, and also shops, restaurants and, for motorists, filling stations. Waterfoot was at one time the centre of an artistic community and the area is still attractive to artists and craft workers.

Carradale golf course with a view of Arran; (inset) Symbols of mortality on an eighteenth-century gravestone at Skipness

Carradale Bay

SADDELL ABBEY

The road south to Campbeltown after Carradale is no longer single-track, but there are steep hills to negotiate at Torrisdale and Saddell, so care is required: more Norse names, which along with Ugadale and Smerby, and the forts of Ifferdale and Guesdale up Saddell Glen, give further evidence of Norse occupation. The first Viking raiders came to Kintyre soon after 800, to be followed by settlers and farmers, with their wives and families. Norse settlement continued unchallenged until the 1150s, though towards the end it is likely that administrative control from Norway was slight. When Somerled staged a revolt against Norse control, and won a sea battle in 1154, the sea kingdom of the Lords of the Isles displaced what was left of Norse rule. He was killed in 1164, but before his death founded a Cistercian abbey at Saddell, intended to show the kings of Scotland that he and his lineage were just as capable of maintaining the trappings of a medieval state.

Somerled died before Saddell Abbey was completed, but his son carried the project forward to fruition, soon after 1200. The remains of this important medieval monastery can still be seen at Saddell, though much has been lost and the site is much in need of explanatory aids so that visitors can appreciate the full size and extent of the Cistercian abbey. There is an impressive collection of late-medieval grave slabs at Saddell – displayed in a shelter which has been compared to a petrol station forecourt. But if their setting is inappropriate, the stones themselves are magnificent. Here are life-size stone warriors, with their javelins, swords and daggers, with chain mail over their chests – and each link of the chain carved in stone. There are also clerics, dressed in ornate ecclesiastical robes. Stones like these are found throughout Kintyre, and indeed throughout the Hebrides and mainland Argyll, but nowhere is there such an impressive collection as

Grave slabs at Saddell Abbey showing medieval warriors and priests

at Saddell. A local pressure group is trying to improve the presentation of the stones, and is working to promote the preservation and interpretation of this site. This is easily the most important ecclesiastical site in Kintyre, and is the religious equivalent of the secular fortress of Skipness – a demonstration of medieval lordly power and prestige. There is a small collection of carved stone fragments from Saddell Abbey in Campbeltown Museum.

SADDELL CASTLE

From Saddell village it is a short walk to Saddell Bay, with Saddell Castle at its western end. This is a tower house built as a residence for the Bishop of Argyll, completed by 1512. By 1650 it had come into the possession of the Campbells, in the shape of the 1st Marquess of Argyll, who leased it to William Ralston of that Ilk – his descendants still live in Kintyre. Towards the end of the seventeenth century it came into the possession of the Campbell lairds of Glensaddell, who quarried stones from Saddell Abbey to build farm steadings around the base of the castle. Part of the enclosing wall of the original castle, the barmkin wall, still survives in the wall of one of these later farm buildings. The Campbells of Saddell built themselves a new house nearby in 1774. The castle gradually fell into disrepair and by the 1970s was derelict. In 1976 it was bought by the Landmark Trust who restored it and furnished it as holiday accommodation.

Both Saddell House and Saddell Castle, and some adjacent properties, are owned by the Landmark Trust, and are not open to the public. However, pedestrian access to the beach at Saddell Bay *is* allowed. Cars must be left at the car park provided, at the main road, beside the gateway to the Saddell estate.

SADDELL IRON AGE HILL FORT

At the east end of Saddell Bay, behind the holiday cottage of Port na Gael, is the Pluck Wood, with both mature beech trees and some remains of native woodland. On the summit of the hill within this wood, overlooking Saddell Bay, are the remains of an Iron Age hill fort, best visited between October and April, when the vegetation is short. The fort probably dates from before 500BC. The single wall of the fort survives best on the east side, facing the sea, where it can be seen as a band of stony debris up to 14ft (4.3m) thick, with two to three courses of the large slabs of the outer face of the wall visible, standing to a height of over 3ft (1m).

Saddell Castle, built for the Bishop of Argyll

KILDONAN GALLERIED DUN

Just three miles south of Saddell, on the road to Campbeltown, is a much more impressive fort, known as Kildonan Galleried Dun. This is a form of Iron Age fortification thought to be intermediate between the simple duns or fortified homesteads which are so common around the coasts of Argyll, and the complex broch towers. The Kildonan dun dates from around AD 200, but was reoccupied in the ninth century, and perhaps again in the medieval period. It was excavated between 1936 and 1939 and produced a wealth of finds, some of which are in Campbeltown Museum. There is a parking place nearby.

KILCHOUSLAND CHAPEL

South of Kildonan is the village of Peninver (in local pronunciation, the second 'n' is not sounded – PenEEver), with a caravan park and sandy beach, suitable for small children. Two miles further on is the farm and church of Kilchousland, another medieval chapel in an attractive setting, with interesting stones in the graveyard. The earliest part of the chapel dates from the twelfth century, but it has been much altered and remodelled, probably in the sixteenth century. The lower part of the shaft of a late-medieval cross from the churchyard at Kilchousland is now in the Campbeltown Museum. Whatever medieval grave-slabs there may have been have not survived, unless they remain buried, but there are several interesting eighteenth-century stones, with carvings and inscriptions. Contrary to popular opinion, the skull and crossbones which appears on several stones is not indicative of either pirates or plague victims, but is simply a symbol of death commonly used in the eighteenth century. The hour-glass is another example of this. There are several carvings of plough teams, and of tools and implements associated with the trade or occupation of the deceased. One headstone has the following epitaph:

SO LET ME LIVE
SO LET ME DIE
YT. I MAY LIVE
ETERNALLIE

Gravestone at Kilchousland

The medieval chapel at Kilchousland, looking across to Arran

Kilchousland chapel is perhaps best visited in the traditional way, by walking to it from Campbeltown, just over 1 mile (1.6km) from the shipyard at Fort Argyll, where cars can be left. There is no room at all for cars to park at Kilchousland, except on the main road, which would be both hazardous and dangerous, as well as inconsiderate. The traffic moves fast on this stretch of road, so even stopping for a quick look is not recommended. Pedestrians approaching the churchyard should be careful to leave all gates securely closed. The walk from Campbeltown is well worth the time and energy, with interesting geology on the shore at Macringan's Point – an interesting name in itself, thought to derive from St Ninian. Kilchousland chapel is dedicated to St Constantine.

Before the road descends into Campbeltown there is a viewpoint, with fine views of the town, Campbeltown Loch and Davaar Island. On a clear day, Ailsa Craig and the coasts of south Ayrshire will be visible. Nearer to hand, the south end of Arran is directly eastwards.

Davaar Island, at the entrance to Campbeltown Loch

Overleaf: The beach at Kilchousland church and Arran

41

3 'THE WEE TOON' – CAMPBELTOWN

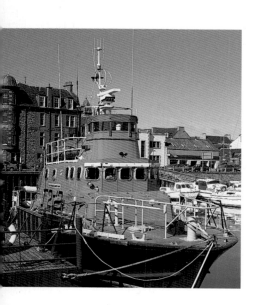

WITH A POPULATION OF 5,600 at the 1991 Census, more than half of all the inhabitants of Kintyre live in Campbeltown, known affectionately as 'The Wee Toon'. The town was founded around 1609 by Archibald, 7th Earl of Argyll, who renamed the existing settlement after his own lineage. Just as in the twentieth century some European place names changed according to which political entity they found themselves in, or according to changes of politics or regime, so at the beginning of the seventeenth century it was a conscious political act to abandon *Ceann loch cille Chiaran*, 'at the head of the loch of St Ciaran', and insist on a new name, which over the years has been spelled variously: Campbelltown, Campbelton, Campbeltoun, with other variations, until in recent times the somewhat illogical 'Campbeltown' has become the standard spelling. There is another 'Campbelltown' in Scotland (the former name for Ardersier, near Inverness) and there is a place of that name in New South Wales, Australia, several in North America, and no doubt elsewhere.

The Gaelic-speaking settlement lay to the south of the present town, near Kilkerran Castle, across the road from Kilkerran Cemetery, with its medieval church on the site of an Early Christian foundation. It is likely that the Campbells built their own castle at the end of their single main street ('High Street') which ran from the harbour up to what is now called Castle Hill. They built a Tolbooth to imprison their enemies and a church for the spiritual needs of the Gaelic-speaking population, in 1642, at the end of Kirk Street. Nothing now remains of this 'Irish Church'. No burial ground is indicated on a plan of around 1760 on which this church is marked, and it is extremely unlikely that there ever was one. Local traditional beliefs that Aidan, a king of Dalriada, was buried at this site are almost certainly mistaken: it is much more likely that if he was indeed buried here it was at the Early Christian site at Kilkerran cemetery.

In the seventeenth century the small number of English-speaking residents of the new town met for worship in what was known as 'the Thatched House' in Kirk Street. Of course, at that time there were dozens of thatched houses in Kintyre, but most of the buildings in the new town would have had slated roofs. At last, in 1706, the Lowlanders built their own stone church, probably on the site of the 'Thatched House'; this is now known as the Kirk Street Hall. Abandoned after 1770, it fell into disrepair,

Left: The harbour at Campbeltown

Bottom left: Campbeltown lifeboat

Below: Campbeltown's main street with the white tower of the Town Hall

Opposite: The still-house at Springbank Distillery, Campbeltown

LOWLANDERS

The introduction of Lowlanders into an entirely Gaelic-speaking, Highland area shows the political agenda of Archibald, 7th Earl of Argyll. The intention was to introduce reliable people into Kintyre, with a Lowland background in farming practices and a Lowland religion – Protestantism. In 1700, the efforts of the Campbells were rewarded by the Establishment when Campbeltown was elevated to the status of a royal burgh, with the advantages for trade and commerce which that implied.

Today, the descendants of the Protestant settlers introduced into Kintyre in the seventeenth century are still well represented in the farms and businesses founded long ago, while the displaced Highland population has never regained its former place in Kintyre society.

and by the end of the nineteenth century was a roofless ruin used by local fishermen to store nets and equipment.

An increase in historical awareness resulted in a campaign to rescue this first Lowland church. Funds were raised, and the building was restored, although no attempt was made to recreate the original interior. The original design was a conventional T-plan, with a central wing at the rear. A stone dated 1904 commemorates the restoration. Relics of the old Gaelic church include a carved stone with the date 1642 and a fine bell dated 1638.

Campbeltown today is a town struggling against its historic past to become a viable community. Its existence at the end of the long peninsula of Kintyre always seems slightly improbable, and there are few remnants of the industries which brought the town prosperity over the last two centuries: fishing, coal-mining and whisky distilling. Farming is still a viable industry – just – due to the fertility of the landscape, and forestry is an important activity, though employing few people. The hope for economic prosperity in Kintyre must be based on small-scale industries, and on tourism, which is increasingly important to the local economy, but insufficiently appreciated by local residents. The efforts of the local enterprise company, Argyll and the Isles Enterprise, and especially the introduction of a ferry service to Antrim in Northern Ireland, augur well for the future.

In its heyday Campbeltown was one of many Clyde coastal resorts, though never one of the biggest. Steamers brought visitors directly from the centre of Glasgow, and until the mid-1930s there was even the 'Wee Train' to whisk them across to Machrihanish for golfing, or just to walk on the beach. How the Tourist Board today must regret the decision, taken on economic grounds, to dispense with the 'Wee Train'!

WHISKY DISTILLERIES

Only one distillery now remains of what was once a major industry in Campbeltown – there were once at least 34. Not very much is known about the early days of whisky distilling in Kintyre, but the few scattered references which do exist give us a tantalising glimpse of a society where *aqua vitae*, in Gaelic *uisge bheatha*, the 'water of life', anglicised to 'whisky', played an important part. For centuries the making of this magical but potent brew was a cottage industry, as common as cheese-making, and just as essential when it came to surviving the long winter months.

In 1636, six quarts (nearly seven litres) of *aqua vitae* were payable by the town of Lochead (Campbeltown) as rent of the farm of Crosshill, though it is not clear whether this was distilled locally. Certainly the preparation of malt, for use in the brewing of ale, was a skill practised for centuries by the farmers of Kintyre. In 1770 Orr, Ballantine and Co. built a brewery near the Town Mill and operated it for about 50 years. A smaller brewery was established in Bolgam Street at about the same time.

Springbank Distillery

The names of maltsters appear in the Lowland church baptismal register and in a 1695 list of burgesses of Campbeltown, so this industry was well established by the late seventeenth century. John Wylie, maltman, was one of the first 12 councillors in office when Campbeltown became a royal burgh in 1700. In 1743, 21 maltsters, all with Lowland names, signed a petition relating to the supply of barley from neighbouring farms. The existence of this malting industry, with as many as 40 malt barns in the town, was an important factor in the growth of distilling on an industrial scale.

By 1713 there was a need for three inspectors in the town, appointed by the Council to ensure that distillers did not sell what was termed 'insufficient stuff' – whisky which had been watered down or weakened. In the *Statistical Account of the Parish of Campbeltown*, published in 1792, the Reverend John Smith tells us that 22 small licensed distillers produced 19,800 gallons a year. In 1782–3, and again in 1795–7, the Commissioners of Supply for Argyll banned the manufacture of whisky and temporarily confiscated all private stills. This was because of the failure of harvests in those years, and the suffering of the poor inhabitants of the burghs of Argyll. It is nothing new to turn to strong drink in times of hardship!

Through the imposition of a harsh licence duty in 1785, it became less and less profitable to make whisky on a small scale, and in 1797 it became an economic impossibility, when the duty was raised to a punitive £9 per gallon of still content. This effectively stopped legal distilling in Campbeltown until 1814–15, when the regulations were revised. Thereafter the duty was levied not on stills but on whisky, at a rate of 9s 4d (47p) per gallon. Illicit distilling continued to be a problem for the government, and in 1823 they reduced the duty on whisky to 2s 4d (12p) per gallon. Illicit distillers then found it impossible to compete against large scale legal whisky production, and conditions were then right for a large and rapid expansion of whisky distilling in Campbeltown.

There were still 20 distilleries in the town in 1860, and this number remained fairly constant until 1920. Thereafter, the industry collapsed. By 1925 there were 12 left, but by 1930 only three, and one of those, Rieclachan, closed in 1934, leaving Springbank and Glen Scotia as the two survivors. Much of our information about the whisky industry of Campbeltown was gathered by Alfred Barnard, who in his 1887 book, *The Whisky Distilleries of the United Kingdom*, gives details of his visit. He stayed at the White Hart Hotel, and managed to visit 21 distilleries, as well as enjoying excursions to Saddell, Glen Lussa and Machrihanish, during a hot, sunny two weeks in July 1886.

As well as providing technical details of production facilities and machinery, Barnard gives many interesting observations about the neighbourhood and its inhabitants. For example, he was particularly taken by Lussa Glen, inland from Peninver: 'famous from time immemorial for the strength, beauty and intelligence of its inhabitants … the appearance and manly bearing of a company of volunteers raised in Glenlussa attracts the admiration of all beholders at Campbeltown, when they visit that town for their weekly drill.' His summary of the town's attractions still holds good today: 'Campbeltown is a pleasant place in summer for those who rejoice in a boundless sea, plenty of boating, fishing and golfing.'

Davaar Island

The Tourist Information Centre at the pier is an essential place for visitors to pick up leaflets about the area, maps, advice on accommodation, and so on. Kintyre has many attractions, and this is the best place to find out about them. The staff are well organised and friendly, and can dispense local advice and sell useful publications (tel: 01586 552056). Most importantly, they can give essential advice on tides for visitors wanting to visit Davaar Island.

The excursion to Davaar Island has become something of a pilgrimage for both locals and visitors, and not just because of the unusual painting in one of its caves. In 1887 some fishermen discovered a painting of the Crucifixion there, and there was consternation in the town – was it a

The Sheriff's Downfall

There is a story told locally of an old lady convicted in the Sheriff Court in Campbeltown of whisky smuggling. Before pronouncing sentence the Sheriff said: 'I dare say, my poor woman, it is not often you have been guilty of this fault.' 'Deed no, Sheriff,' the old lady replied, 'I haena made a drop since youn wee keg I sent to yersel.'

Davaar Island, at the entrance to Campbeltown Loch

Opposite: The cave painting on Davaar Island

LIBRARY HISTORY

Inside the public library can still be seen the original 'indicator boards', which told the public whether books were available or out on loan. Access to the book stacks was for library staff only; the public consulted a printed catalogue, checked the number of an item on the indicator board, then asked staff for that book. 'Browsing' was not allowed.

Books were stored on two levels in the area now used for the local history collections – hence the low ceiling and the quaint cast-iron spiral staircase in the corner of the room. Heating in the reading rooms was by open fires supplemented by ancient radiators. The entrance hall originally contained special stands for reading newspapers, which had to be read standing up.

miracle? Eventually it was discovered to be the work of a local art teacher, Alexander MacKinnon. He returned to Kintyre in his old age in the 1930s to re-touch his cave painting, and from time to time, over the years since, local people have maintained its appearance.

There is a line of seven caves in the great cliffs of Davaar – the cave painting is in the fifth of them. Access to Davaar Island is possible only at low tide, across a shingle causeway, An Dorlinn, an easy walk of almost a mile. However, when the tide turns it comes in fast, so it is essential to pay attention to the tide times. Once on Davaar Island, the walk to the caves is over rough boulders on the shore, and not suitable for those who are infirm or unfit. This part of the walk takes about half an hour each way. There is time to explore the rest of Davaar – some farm steadings, the lighthouse, and the lighthouse keepers' houses.

CAMPBELTOWN MUSEUM

Back in Campbeltown, there is an excellent little museum housed in the handsome sandstone building on the front, facing the harbour. Campbeltown Public Library and Museum is in a building donated in 1898 by James Macalister Hall of Killean, designed by the eminent Scottish architect Sir John James Burnet. Beneath the striking cupola is an attractive entrance hall with engraved glass. Externally, a frieze depicts local industries. The interior has been rearranged since the days when there was no public access to the books and separate reading rooms for ladies and gentlemen. There is an excellent local history collection in the library, and the museum, recently renovated, has important material of local interest including archaeological artefacts of national importance: a Bronze Age jet necklace and Neolithic pottery from the chambered cairn at Beacharr.

HERITAGE CENTRE AND PICTURE HOUSE

In the Lorne Street Church, known as 'the Tartan Kirk' partly from its Gaelic associations but mainly from the striped appearance of its exterior caused by alternating red and yellow sandstone, is the Campbeltown Heritage Centre, a treasure house of memorabilia about Campbeltown's former days. A visit to this interesting and informative heritage centre is highly recommended. Built in 1868 to replace the Gaelic Free and English Free churches that previously stood together on this site, the church closed in 1990 when the congregation amalgamated with the Longrow church. The handsome Castlehill church, dating from 1778–80, closed in 1971 and in 1986 was converted to residential flats. Clearly the present population of Campbeltown is not as religious as its predecessors.

Also recommended is a visit to the Campbeltown Picture House, known as 'The Wee Pictures' to distinguish it from its former neighbour, the Rex, now demolished. Dating from 1913, it is the earliest purpose-built

cinema in Scotland, despite occasional claims from metropolitan impostors, and is probably the oldest surviving cinema still showing films. Its distinctive Art Nouveau architecture clashes rather with the sandstone library building next door – but integrated planning has never been a feature of Campbeltown's architecture, especially on the seafront. The building was extensively renovated internally in 1988.

CAMPBELTOWN CROSS

There are many other buildings and churches of interest around Campbeltown which the visitor can explore at leisure with the assistance of pamphlets and leaflets from the Tourist Office. However, the most impressive monument in the town is not the War Memorial, built on reclaimed land at the head of Campbeltown Loch, but the medieval Campbeltown Cross, a masterpiece of carving, situated in the middle of a traffic roundabout at the bottom of Main Street. Formerly it stood in the middle of the road in front of the Town Hall, but during the War was removed for safety and re-erected in its present position in 1945.

The Campbeltown Cross is carved in detailed interlocking knot and foliage designs, with an inscription dating it to around 1380. It was brought to the town to function as a market cross around 1680, most likely from the medieval church and graveyard at Kilkivan, near Machrihanish. It was probably carved at Saddell Abbey, in one of the workshops scattered round Argyll working under the patronage of the Lords of the Isles – the others were at Iona, Oronsay, Kilmartin and Archattan. Unfortunately, the Campbeltown Cross was mutilated, carefully, at the time of the Protestant Reformation, because it depicted the Crucifixion, Mary sitting on a throne holding the infant Jesus, and a priest. Evidently the Reformers approved of mermaids, for they left her image intact.

Campbeltown is a busy market town and administrative centre, with a full range of services and shops. There is a regular bus service to Glasgow, daily flights to Glasgow Airport from the nearby airport, and a summer ferry service to Northern Ireland. The paddle steamer *Waverley* visits occasionally during the summer. There are good facilities for visiting yachts and an active yachting club.

Campbeltown Cross and (right) the paddle steamer, Waverley

4 THE SOUTH END

CIARAN'S FONT

St Ciaran's Cave contains a plain stone font or basin, and a decorated boulder which bears a circular incised T-fret decorative border enclosing a six-petalled 'marigold' pattern; this is a typical Early Christian design, created by the play of compasses within a circle. It occurs on Early Christian stone and metalwork in Ireland, the Isle of Man and in other parts of Scotland.

THERE ARE TWO WAYS of getting from Campbeltown to the south tip of Kintyre: by the fast, direct route down the middle of the peninsula, or by the more leisurely road down the east side. By the direct route the village of Southend is 10 miles (16km) south of Campbeltown: take the Machrihanish road out of Campbeltown and turn left at Stewarton. The alternative, scenic route leaves the town by way of Kilkerran cemetery, past the new Irish ferry terminal. The road winds round Campbeltown Loch, passing Davaar Island. Just at the point where the road turns inland and climbs steeply uphill, it is possible to park and walk along the shore, through the lands of Kildalloig, past the old cottage named New Orleans, towards Auchinhoan Head.

ST CIARAN'S CAVE

Just before the point of the headland are some caves, in one of which are relics of St Ciaran, the Irish saint who gave Campbeltown its original Gaelic name. He was a contemporary of St Columba, one of a band of early Christian missionaries who brought a new religion to Argyll in the sixth century. At the same time, their secular counterparts brought a new political system to the region – the kingdom of Dalriada. These Irish immigrants brought with them a new language, Gaelic.

The walk to the cave is best attempted at low tide and is not easy, although no climbing is involved. The shore is covered with large boulders, and progress can be slow; a lot of scrambling and clambering is required. When the tide is low the walk takes about half an hour from New Orleans. Do not be tempted to approach or leave the caves by climbing the cliffs above.

BALNABRAID GLEN

The Leerside road leaves the shore and climbs steeply to avoid Auchinhoan Head, then rejoins the coast, after a series of hairpin bends, at the entrance to Balnabraid Glen, at a place known locally as the Second Waters, a favourite picnic spot. A walk up the glen is most rewarding – look out for the deserted ruins of houses abandoned long ago. There is a large Bronze Age burial cairn beside the road, excavated in 1910, 1913 and again in 1966, the last because the cairn is being eroded by the stream which runs beside it. The remains of 12 burial cists were found in this cairn, some of them containing pottery and cremations in the typical Bronze Age style. Dating evidence suggests the site was in use from 1700–1500BC.

Leaving the Second Waters, the road climbs up high again, giving excellent views across the Firth of Clyde. Occasionally basking sharks can be seen in the coastal waters far below. After crossing some high moorland the road drops down to the fertile farmlands of Southend. Visitors interested in prehistory may wish to explore the chambered cairn of Blasthill, with a reasonably well-preserved outline and crescentic forecourt. Out to sea, the island of Sanda is visible, with an Early Christian chapel dedicated to St Ninian, and an early cross.

DUNAVERTY CASTLE

Southend is a small village with a shop, hotel, filling station and two very important historic sites: a castle and a church. The castle of Dunaverty lay to the south of the village on the precipitous headland jutting out into the sea, which overlooks the excellent links golf course. It has had a long and bloody history, culminating in the tragic events of 1647, when the royalist garrison of 300 men surrendered and was massacred by the Covenanting army of General David Leslie, at the instigation of his chaplain. The dead were buried in the enclosure which stands in a field near the village.

The fortress of Dunaverty first comes on record in the *Annals of Ulster* for AD712, when it was besieged by Sealbach, King of Dalriada. It was captured by King Haakon of Norway in 1263, sheltered Robert the Bruce in 1306 and was visited by James IV in 1494. According to local tradition, Sir John MacDonald of Dunnivaig hanged the newly installed royal governor over the castle walls as the king sailed away, but this may have been wishful

Left: Columba's chapel, Southend, looking across to Dunaverty and Sanda

ANGUS MACVICAR

Overlooking the beach at Southend is the home of Angus MacVicar, a prolific writer of children's books and for children's radio in the early part of his career. More recently, this son of the manse has produced a series of best-selling books of autobiographical memories and local yarns, of which Salt in my Porridge *was the first.*

Entertaining stories of the minister's salmon and of exploits on the local golf course breeching NATO security at the height of the Cold War are intermingled with a couthy and perceptive commentary on Kintyre society.

thinking as there is no corroborative documentation and it seems unlikely that such an act would have been ignored or gone unpunished and unrecorded. The castle was rebuilt in 1542, attacked by the Earl of Sussex during his raid on Kintyre in 1558, and demolished in 1685, after the forfeiture of the Earl of Argyll. Today only slight traces of walling remain. The site is easily approached by the track leading to the Dunaverty golf club, but care is required.

St Columba's Chapel

The medieval parish church at Southend is Kilcolmkill, or St Columba's chapel. The medieval church was built under the patronage of the Lords of the Isles, probably in the 1320s. It lies beside the main road, about a mile to the west of the village of Southend. The east end of the ruin dates from the thirteenth century; the rest is later. From some decorative carved stones built into the fabric of the chapel it can be deduced that there was an earlier stone church of Romanesque design on the same site, dating from the twelfth century.

About 20yd (18m) north-west of the north-west corner of the church was a well, on the north side of the old road passing the northern boundary of the graveyard. There is an incised Latin cross on the rock face above the well.

Medieval grave-slabs and fragments lie inside the church and in the surrounding graveyard. These all date from the period 1350–1500, and were carved in Kintyre, probably at Saddell Abbey, under the patronage of the Lords of the Isles. One of the slabs has a particularly fine carving of a medieval galley with furled sails, rigging and a hinged rudder, with a shield in the prow and a banner in the stern.

The area around Southend has always been important in the history of Kintyre, and some of the seventeenth and eighteenth century stones at Kilcolmkill reflect this. Just outside the east wall of the church is a slab in memory of Ranald McDonald of Sanda who died in 1681, at the age of 34, and his wife, Anna Stewart, who died in 1722 at the age of 74; the stone bears the family crest. Ranald McDonald was an infant, a babe in arms, at the time of the massacre at Dunaverty in 1647; his nurse pleaded for his life and he was spared. This old Kintyre family traces its descent from the Lords of the Isles, who controlled Kintyre until 1475.

Against the inner face of the east wall of the church is the headstone of Neil McNeil of Carskey, who died in 1685; the stone bears the family crest and motto – VINCIT AUT MORI[?TUR] – 'He either conquers or dies'. The McNeils of Carskey lived in the area for many centuries. The Compt book (account book) of Malcolm McNeil of Carskey, covering the years 1703–1743, has survived and has been reprinted.

The rock of Dunaverty, scene of a siege and massacre in 1647

ST COLUMBA'S FOOTPRINTS

Overlooking the medieval chapel at Southend, on a rocky outcrop, two footprints are carved into the rock, known as 'St Columba's Footprints' (illustrated right). One of the footprints is known to have been carved by a local stonemason in 1856, but the other, nearest Ireland, is ancient and perhaps was used in the inauguration of kings, who would promise to follow in the footsteps of their ancestors. Here we are well aware of our Irish origins; the coastline of Antrim, the ancestral homeland of all Gaels, is only 15 miles (24km) away across the North Channel and is usually clearly visible.

St Columba sailed for Iona in AD563, and is thought to have landed in Kintyre to pay his respects to the secular rulers of Argyll, which at that time was a newly established colony of Gaelic-speaking settlers, or at any rate the territory of a ruling class of Gaelic speakers from Antrim – probably, as with most 'invasions', the local population were little affected by the political events swirling around them. A church service is held at 'the Footprints' every year to commemorate Columba's visit. A signposted track leads from near the car park beside Keil Caves. Excavations in the largest cave in the 1930s showed that it was lived in during the Dalriadic period; the finds are in Campbeltown Museum.

The outline of a rectangular building below the footprints to the west may be all that remains of an

(Continued opposite)

The Ralston Monument, at the west end of the churchyard, standing against the north wall of the burial enclosure, bears the family crest and commemorates William Ralston of that Ilk, the Ayrshire laird who was the leader of the Lowland Plantation of Kintyre in the seventeenth century; he died in 1691. A recumbent slab in the churchyard, dated 1697, commemorates Anna Hamilton, the wife of Thomas Maxwell. It bears the crest of each family. Nearby stones relate to other members of the Maxwell family, who played a leading part in the Lowland Plantation.

Two headstones dated 1799 and 1805 have fine carvings of plough teams, while there is a fine carving of a fully rigged sailing ship on a stone erected by Alexander McKenzie, mariner, in memory of his mother, who died in 1847. A stone erected by David Campbell, shepherd in the Mull of Kintyre, in memory of his son who died in 1789, has very worn carvings.

ARCHAEOLOGICAL SITES

There are many archaeological sites around Southend, as in other parts of Kintyre, but two sites are worthy of mention. The largest hill fort in Kintyre is on the hill of Cnoc Araich behind Southend Primary School. Access is from the track leading to High Machrimore farm; the farmer should be consulted before proceeding up to the fort. Measuring 224yds (204m) by 194yds (177m), and thus enclosing an area of 6.25 acres (2.5ha), it is not on a position of great natural strength, relying for its defence on three ramparts of earth and stone, with associated ditches. The ramparts were never very substantial, so it may be that building strong defences was not a major consideration for these Iron Age builders; perhaps the size and prestige of the site were the most important features. It has been suggested that this is the tribal capital of the *Epidii* or 'horse people'; from the ancient Greek geographer Ptolemy we know they lived in Kintyre when the Roman fleet passed by around AD82.

On the cliff edge overlooking Sron Uamha, which is the most southerly promontory of Kintyre, there is a well-preserved fort, defended by three stone walls. Access is difficult, over 1 mile (1.8km) of rough ground from the road leading to the Mull of Kintyre lighthouse, but the site is well worth a visit. On a clear day there is a spectacular view across the North Channel to the coasts of Antrim.

Towards 200BC Iron Age folk in Kintyre changed their style of living, abandoning the hill-top forts of their ancestors for smaller, family-size structures. These are known as 'duns', and are typically sited on coastal promontories or rocky knolls, relying for defence on the use of natural features and a dry-stone wall 13–17½ft (4–5m) in height and 7–10ft (2–3m) wide, usually with a well-designed entrance. They may have housed 10–15 people, living in lean-to structures built against the inner walls, leaving the unroofed centre free for cooking.

One of the finest duns in Kintyre overlooks the mouth of Borgadel Water, west of Southend. It is a circular structure, 43ft (13m) in diameter, with a wall up to 13ft (4m) thick and a well-preserved entrance. The wall survives to a maximum height of 6ft (1.8m). The stone-walled structure in the interior is the remains of a later sheepfold. Access is difficult to this remote site, which is undoubtedly why it is so well preserved. The best approach is along the road leading to the Mull of Kintyre lighthouse, walking down Borgadel Glen.

MULL OF KINTYRE LIGHTHOUSE

Made famous by Paul McCartney's 1977 hit single, the Mull of Kintyre is, strictly speaking, the rounded headland making up the south-west corner of the Kintyre peninsula. Since 1788 a lighthouse has warned shipping to keep well away from an area notorious for its tidal currents and turbulent seas. The complex has been re-modelled several times; the keepers' houses date from 1857 and 1883. An early reflecting mechanism from the lighthouse is in the Campbeltown Museum.

From Southend, the lighthouse is 8 miles (12.9km) along a single-track road, which climbs eventually to 1,350ft (412m) before descending nearly 1,000ft (305m) in three-quarters of a mile, with fearsome hairpin bends. Vehicles must be left at the car park at the top of the hill, overlooking the lighthouse, which stands on the edge of a 300ft (92m) cliff. In 1994 a Chinook helicopter carrying security personnel from Northern Ireland

(continued)
early Christian chapel, possibly established by Columba himself, since the medieval chapel is dedicated to him. In the distance the island of Sanda reminds us that Columba was not the first to bring Christianity to Kintyre, for there the chapel dedication is to St Ninian of Whithorn. It is now thought that St Ninian died in the first quarter of the sixth century, though traditionally his date of death was given as 422. A date of about a hundred years later than that now seems more likely. We have already encountered Ninian at the entrance to Campbeltown Loch, at Macringan's Point.

There is another example of a footprint carved on a rock in Argyll at Dunadd, near Lochgilphead, thought to be the most important fortress of the Kingdom of Dalriada. However, if as is thought, this was a 'peripatetic' kingship, where the king progressed around his territories from one fort to another, collecting tribute, it is quite likely that inauguration ceremonies were carried out at more than one place. There is also a tradition of a 'footprint stone' at Finlaggan, in Islay, where the Lords of the Isles were inaugurated.

Between Southend and Kilcolmkill, below the white concrete edifice of the former Keil Hotel, are the ruins of Keil School, a private educational establishment for the sons of Argyll, established by Sir William Mackinnon, who made his fortune in East Africa. It burned down in 1924 and was relocated in Dumbarton, where it still flourishes.

to a conference at Fort George, near Inverness, inexplicably flew straight into the Mull of Kintyre, in cloudy conditions, killing all 29 people on board. A memorial cairn commemorates the victims.

BALVICAR

Several other aircraft wrecks from earlier years lie on the nearby hills. A mile north of the lighthouse, along a rough and overgrown track, lie the ruins of the abandoned township of Balvicar, one of several on this exposed coastline between the Mull and Machrihanish. The remains of many structures can be seen at Balvicar: houses, out-buildings, byres and enclosures, not all of the same age. It was tenanted in the seventeenth century, but was deserted by 1779. Near the best-preserved house is a 'horizontal' water mill, or clack mill. There are also traces of a corn-drying kiln attached to a byre.

Local residents are irritated by the misuse of the term 'Mull of Kintyre' which in the interests of the tourist industry is now used, ridiculously, to include places as far north as Tarbert. When locals speak of 'The Mull' they mean the headland on which the lighthouse stands.

The memorial cairn on the Mull of Kintyre, commemorating the 1994 helicopter crash

Below: Above the Mull of Kintyre lighthouse

5 THE LAGGAN

TO THE WEST OF Campbeltown is a triangular area of low-lying ground, known as the Laggan. It is bounded by Machrihanish to the west, Westport to the north, and Campbeltown to the east. After the end of the last Ice Age, as recently as 10,000 years ago, the Laggan would have been flooded by sea water, making the Mull of Kintyre into the headland of a detached island. Gradually the waters receded and the land rose slightly, leaving an inhospitable and impenet-rable triangle, covered with dense scrub where the drainage was good, but otherwise boggy.

After the climatic deterioration around 1200BC, the trees rotted and it became an area of marshes and peat moss. The Laggan has now been drained and largely cleared of peat, though some peat banks still remain and are cut locally for fuel on a small scale. The agricultural land is

Below and overleaf: Coastal waters in Machrihanish Bay

61

extremely fertile, providing excellent grain crops and superlative grazing for dairy herds.

Much of the west side of the Laggan is now within the perimeter of the now mothballed RAF Machrihanish. A NATO runway of over 10,000ft (3,050m) can accommodate the world's most advanced aircraft. The closure of this base, and the withdrawal of the American special forces who were based there, had a devastating economic impact on Campbeltown and south Kintyre. The runway is still used for civilian flights and there is a terminal building to service passengers travelling to Glasgow or Islay.

BRONZE AGE CAIRNS

Two Bronze Age cairns can be visited at Machrihanish. One lies at the east edge of the village on the south side of the main road from Campbeltown: known locally as Cnocan Sithein ('fairy hill') it is 78ft (24m) in diameter and 11ft (3.5m) in height – quite an imposing monument. It was explored in the 1820s and found to contain only an incomplete adult skeleton in a stone cist, covered by a massive cap-stone. The cairn was of composite construction, consisting of a core of stone and an outer casing of sand, earth and turf. On the other side of the village, on the east side of Uisaid promontory, there is a round cairn, grass-covered. It is possible to trace the larger kerb stones around the south edge of the cairn.

IRON AGE HILL FORTS

During the Iron Age, from 850BC to AD200 the hills around the Laggan were protected by a series of hill forts. On the north side, the forts at Largiemore, Ranachan Hill, Ballywilline Hill and Knock Scalbert are all impressive, easily accessible and well worth a visit. On the south side of the Laggan the fort on Bealloch Hill guards the pass to Southend from which it takes its name. From all of these sites there are spectacular views over the flat land of the Laggan.

Bealloch Hill is the only one of these to have been excavated. It produced a major surprise when two Bronze Age cremation burials were found sealed beneath a rampart. One of the cremation urns contained a bronze chisel and a tiny pottery vessel known as an incense or 'pygmy' cup. The fort at Bealloch Hill had three ramparts and ditches; access is from the Southend road below.

Graveslabs at Kilkivan churchyard near Machrihanish

KILKIVAN CHAPEL

There are two medieval chapels in the Laggan, both with sculptured stones, at Kilkivan and Kilchenzie. Kilkivan is near Machrihanish; Kilchenzie is on the main A83 Campbeltown road. From the chapel at Kilkivan there are fine views over the Laggan to Islay and Jura. This site is of particular interest because it appears that the Campbeltown Cross originated here, and was taken to the town in the seventeenth century to serve as a market cross. The Latin inscription, in 'Lombardic capitals', suggests that the cross was made around 1380 and, from the design, probably in Iona:

HEC EST CRVX D	This is the cross of
OMINI YUARI MH	Sir Yvarus [Ivor]
EACHYRNA QVOND	MacEachern, sometime
AM RECTORIS DE	parson of
KYLKECAN ET DO	Kylkecan [Kilkivan]
MINI ANDREE NAT	and of Sir Andreas [Andrew]
I EIVS RECTORIS	his son, parson
DE KILCOMAN Q	of Kilchoman [in Islay], who
VI HANC CRVCEM	caused this cross
FIERI FACIEBAT	to be made

Because he was the son of a priest and an unmarried woman, Andrew MacEachern had to apply for a special dispensation to serve as a priest, because of his 'defect of birth'. From surviving records in the Vatican archives we know that Andrew, following in his father's footsteps, had been the parson at Kilkivan 'for many years' when in 1375 he moved to Kilchoman in Islay to become the parson there. In 1382 Andrew's right to hold Kilchoman was challenged on the grounds that he should have applied for a new dispensation when he moved to the new parish, and he was dispossessed and replaced. The Campbeltown Cross must therefore date to the period 1375–82, when Andrew MacEachern was the parson of Kilchoman.

INDUSTRIAL ARCHAEOLOGY

Coal must have been found in the Carboniferous outcrops on the south side of the Laggan from very early times. The first record is in 1498, when James IV

TRANSATLANTIC WIRELESS

There is more industrial archaeology in Machrihanish – the remains of a wireless station. On 1 January 1906 a direct Transatlantic wireless telegraphy link between Machrihanish and Massachusetts was achieved by Professor Reginald A. Fessenden of the National Signalling Company of Washington, D.C. The transmitting tower that was used in these experiments was 450ft (137m) high, composed of steel tubing 5ft (1.5m) in diameter, inside which were maintenance ladders. Resting on a ball and socket device, it was held in place by wire guy ropes, anchored in massive concrete blocks in the ground.

The telegraphic messages were sent across the Atlantic for three days to a similar station at Brant Rock, north of Boston, Massachusetts. Contact was then
(continued opposite)

employed John Davidson, 'a collman, to pass through Kintyre to verify if colys may be wonnyn there'. Perhaps Laggan coal warmed his royal castles in Kintyre, at Dunaverty, Kilkerran, Skipness and Tarbert. With the growth of the burgh of Campbeltown there was a ready market for local coal, which was carted to the town for use in distilleries. This was the great age of canal building throughout Britain, and in 1773 James Watt surveyed a route for a canal to bring coal from Drumlemble to Campbeltown. Construction began in 1783, and the canal was in operation by 1794. It terminated close to the site of the town gasworks, at the north end of Glebe Street. The canal was 3 miles (4.8km) long, with no locks. Coal was transported in barges carrying 40 cartloads a day to Campbeltown.

By 1856 the canal was little used, and when the colliery at Drumlemble changed hands in 1875 the Coal Canal was found to be choked with weeds. The new Argyll Coal and Canal Co. decided to join the Railway Age. The new line was operational by May 1877. From the Coal Ree – the coal depot – in Campbeltown to the pits at Drumlemble was just over 4 miles (6.4km). In 1881 the line was extended half a mile (0.8km) further westwards to the Argyll Colliery, the new pits being opened at Kilkivan. In 1897 the Campbeltown Coal Company took over, and responded to the new tourist industry which disgorged large numbers of day trippers in Campbeltown from the steamers *King Edward* and *Queen Alexandra*. In 1904 the Campbeltown and Machrihanish Light Railway Company came into being, and gained permission to extend the railway along Hall Street in Campbeltown to a new terminus opposite the Christian Institute, near where the Cross now stands. At the other end, the line was extended from the coal pits to a terminus in Machrihanish opposite the Ugadale Arms Hotel. The new line opened in 1906.

Throughout most of its life the railway ran three trains a day in each direction, with extra trains on Saturdays and 'express trains' connecting with the steamers, whisking passengers across to the delights of Machrihanish with its hotel, golf course and magnificent beach in only 20 minutes. Day trippers could spend a full 35 minutes on the Atlantic coast before they had to rejoin the 'Wee Train' to catch their steamer.

Cleaning halibut tanks at the Marine Environmental Research Laboratory

The closure of the Argyll Colliery in 1929 meant the end of the railway age in Kintyre. The line could no longer survive, and closed in 1931, a victim of the efficiency of the internal combustion engines in McConnachie's blue buses.

CRAIGAIG

South of the remains of the Wireless Telegraphy Station is the bay known as The Gauldrons, with strange rock formations, a sandy beach, and a great variety of pebbles. One mile (1.6km) further on, along a coastal path, is the deserted settlement of Craigaig (locally pronounced 'krajak'). The stony ruins of cottages and farm buildings of several periods can be seen at Craigaig. Between here and the Mull of Kintyre was a string of isolated coastal settlements joined together by a cart track, which can still be followed for long stretches. Unfortunately, the growth of bracken in the summer months makes it almost impossible to find this track.

The economy of these townships was probably based on flax, which was taken to the Lint Mill just outside Campbeltown. After the Napoleonic Wars this industry collapsed, and it appears that most of the Mull of Kintyre coastal villages were abandoned by about 1830 and the whole area given over to sheep. Herds of wild goats are sometimes seen on this coast, no doubt the descendants of stock abandoned when the last residents left. Further south the ruins of Iron Age forts testify to subsistence agriculture on this coast from prehistoric times. It must always have been a harsh environment, with only tiny pockets of land flat enough to cultivate. All the coastal settlements are favoured with streams or fresh water and suitable beaches for fishing boats.

Craigaig is the most accessible of these townships, but care should be taken not to intrude on the fields of the farm of Ballygreggan by keeping close to the cliff edge as far as possible. Cars should not be taken along the Ballygreggan road. The walk from Craigaig to the Mull of Kintyre lighthouse is spectacular and rewarding, but extremely demanding over very rough terrain, requiring a full day for fit and experienced walkers, and not to be undertaken lightly.

Up until the early nineteenth century there was a small-scale salt industry at Machrihanish, which some locals still refer to as 'The Pans'. Today the foreshore is completely changed: car parks and the installation of water and sewerage pipes have removed all traces of the areas where salt water was trapped and salt recovered through evaporation.

(continued)
unaccountably broken, and apart from one other successful transmission three weeks later, Fessenden was unable to develop his equipment. It now appears that his success was due to freak weather conditions, as his transmitting gear put out too weak a signal to be of any value in normal circumstances.

The tower blew down in a horrific north-westerly gale on 5 December 1906. Fortunately, its 70 tons of steel missed the machinery house, where two workmen were having their lunch. Traces of the concrete blocks which anchored the wires can still be seen, and the concrete foundations of buildings are still visible. Great secrecy was maintained during the experiments, giving rise to speculation that Fessenden was a German spy. He never achieved the fame of his rival, Marconi. He also developed a device for superimposing the human voice on high frequency radio signals, but this was never installed at Machrihanish and his only brief success was in telegraphy.

The ruins of Fessenden's experiment are in Losset Low Park, south of the old lifeboat station, now a marine research laboratory, at Uisaid Point.

6 THE WEST SIDE

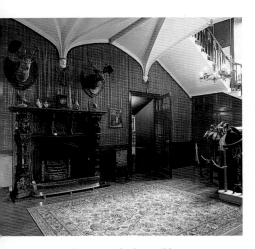

Hallway in Glenbarr Abbey

THE MAIN A83 ROAD out of Campbeltown heads north-west, skirting the northern edge of the triangle of the Laggan and hitting the west coast at Westport. A large car park here invites visitors to spend some time on the beach. This is where locals come to swim and surf in hot summers, but care is required, as the beach is steep and with dangerous undertows. The beach is a full 3 miles (5km) long, sandy for the most part, and full of interest. Where it is a little pebbly there are often examples of 'sea coal' to be found, presumably washed out from underwater outcrops of coalbearing Carboniferous deposits. There is always an interesting selection of driftwood, and on many visits no other human beings will be encountered. There are superb views of the coastline of the Mull of Kintyre to the south and, to the north-west, the hills of Islay and the Paps of Jura. In clear weather, far off to the south-west is the coastline of Northern Ireland.

Heading north, the road, much improved in recent years, hugs the western coastline of Kintyre. After Bellochantuy, a place which gives visitors much difficulty in its pronunciation (something like 'byellochan-TEE'), the road follows the raised beach, left high and dry by changes in sea level after the last Ice Age. There are at least ten Iron Age forts and duns between Westport and Glenbarr, including one which was excavated in the 1960s. The finds suggested a date in the second century AD and an occupation lasting intermittently for five or six centuries. The dun occupies the summit of a rock stack some 35ft (10m) in height; it measures about 44ft (13.4m) by 19ft (5.8m) within a drystone wall varying in thickness from nearly 10ft (3m) near the entrance to 4ft (1.2m) elsewhere.

GLENBARR ABBEY

The main road by-passes the village of Glenbarr, but it is worth taking the short detour through the village to visit Glenbarr Abbey, which is not an abbey at all but a rather ostentatious mansion house. These are the lands of the Macalisters of Glenbarr, and it is worth driving up the glen as far as the road goes to experience the sheltered fertility of a typical Kintyre glen. Visitors interested in archaeology can pick up a leaflet locally or at the Tourist Information Centre in Campbeltown which gives details of cup-and-ring markings on several rock outcrops in the area. These are thought

to date from the Bronze Age. Walkers can continue up Barr Glen to the ridge of Kintyre, to climb Beinn an Turc 1,490ft (454m), the highest hill in Kintyre. Glenbarr Abbey contains a small museum of family memorabilia which will be of interest to Macalisters.

Beacharr standing stone, the tallest in Kintyre. In 1792 the local minister called it 'a curious monument of the knowledge which our forefathers must have had of the mechanic powers'

MUASDALE

The next little west coast village north of Glenbarr is Muasdale, its Norse name derived from *mungas-dalr*, the valley of the monks. The reference is to Saddell Abbey, and there is a tradition that when King Haakon of Norway was anchored with his fleet between the off-shore islands of Gigha and Cara, his chaplain died and the body was taken ashore at Muasdale, to be carried through the glens and over the hills for burial at Saddell. The village has a caravan park and general store.

KILLEAN

Three miles (4.8km) further north is the estate village of Killean, its architecture jarring with other local buildings. Killean House stands hidden in the trees above. Nearby is the standing stone at Beacharr, the tallest in

Kintyre – 16¹/₂ft (5.03m). Beside it is a Neolithic chambered cairn, famous in the history of archaeology as the first plase where domestic Neolithic pottery was recognised, with its distinctive round-based shapes. The original pottery from Beacharr chambered cairn is in the Campbeltown Museum. These sites are worth visiting.

Also in Killean is the most important medieval parish church in Kintyre, taking its name from St John, to whom it is dedicated. Here again is evidence of the power and patronage, and immense wealth, of the Lords of the Isles. No expense was spared in bringing the best ecclesiastical architects to Kintyre to design and build these churches. Killean church is in rather a sorry state, threatened by ivy, robbed of some of its dressed stones, its windows blocked up – but enough remains of superb architectural detail to realise that this was an important church. The oldest part is the nave, built as a modest chapel in the second half of the twelfth century. Early in the thirteenth century the church was extended to the east and a new and elaborate chancel added. The double window in the east gable is especially fine. During the fifteenth century an aisle was added to the north side of the chancel. In due course it became the family burial vault of the MacDonalds of Largie. The vault, which is usually locked, contains a collection of late-medieval gravestones. The church continued in use after the Reformation but was abandoned in 1770, when a new church was built on the promontory of A'Chleit, 2 miles (3km) to the south.

The ruined church at Killean, near Tayinloan

Opposite: Medieval graveslabs in the Largie vault

Above: Sunset over the Paps of Jura from Ronachan. Cora Bheinn is on the right

Right: Ronachan Bay

Pages 74–75: The view from Dun Skeig to Islay and the Paps of Jura

RHUNAHAORINE POINT

Just under a mile north of Killean is the village of Tayinloan, with a general store and old inn. On the shore below the village is a ferry slipway, from which Caledonian MacBrayne run a car and passenger ferry to the island of Gigha. North of Tayinloan is Rhunahaorine Point, a shingle spit jutting out into the Sound of Gigha. The shingle beaches make a strange landscape, well worth a visit. The road goes as far as a caravan site, located on the beach. There are restful walks in extensive pine woods. The road to Rhunahaorine turns off the infamous 'Tayinloan straight', an almost perfectly straight stretch of road for 3 miles (4.8km), over which local traffic often travels far too fast. Towards the north end of this stretch, on the west side of the road, is what looks like the control tower of an airport. Here, during the Second World War, a dummy airfield was built, complete with dummy aircraft, to confuse the Germans.

BALLOCHROY STANDING STONES AND CORRIECHREVIE

Just after the A83 hits the coast again, at the end of the Tayinloan straight, is the farm of Ballochroy. Turning up the first farm track north of Ballochroy Farm leads to the famous standing stones at Ballochroy, a line of three stones supposedly aligned astronomically in two directions. To the south-west, a sight-line over Cara Island marks midwinter sunset, while to the north-west, one of the stones appears to be aligned on the Paps of Jura, or at least on Cora Bheinn, the mountain to the north (right) of the Paps. It marks the midsummer sunset. Some archeo-astronomers believe that these stones, and others, were used to fix the calendar very exactly, allowing the possibility of eclipse prediction for both the sun and the moon.

Just a mile north of Ballochroy another farm track leads to the magnificent cairn of Corriechrevie, apparently still largely intact and unexcavated. We see so many ruined, not to say tenuous, cairns in Scottish archaeology, that it comes as a welcome surprise to find one which allows us to gauge something of the impressiveness it would have caused in the Bronze Age.

It is worth pausing at the viewpoint at Ronachan Point, for there are usually seals arranged on the off-shore skerries. The large mound just in front of the car park is a ruinous Iron Age dun. In the woods above Ronachan House, a Church of Scotland residential home, is an earlier Iron Age fort, so there are two forts of different types and different dates, though both Iron Age, only a short distance apart.

CLACHAN

However, at Dun Skeig, overlooking the village of Clachan, 2 miles (3km) north of Ronachan, there is a magnificent Iron Age site, with no less than three forts on the same hill top. This is really worth visiting, if only for the magnificent view up West Loch Tarbert, across to Knapdale, and westwards to Islay and Jura. It is possible to get quite close to Dun Skeig along a farm track, before crossing rough ground and scrambling up the hill. The oldest fort is a single stone wall encompassing most of the hilltop; next is a ruinous circular dun, with some sections vitrified, at the south end of the hill; and last is a well-preserved dun at the north end of the hilltop.

Left: Clachan churchyard, angel

Medieval graveslabs in Clachan churchyard

Fragments in the graveyard of the church at Clachan hint at an Early Christian chapel on this site, presumably underneath the eighteenth-century building. There are also carved late-medieval graveslabs here. Just outside the village to the north is Balnakill House, built by Sir William Mackinnon (1823–93). Born in Campbeltown, he made his fortune in the shipping trade, eventually as the owner of the British India Steam Navigation Company. He established himself in East Africa and was commemorated by a statue in Mombasa, before it was taken down after Tanzania became independent and returned to his native land. It now stands outside Keil School in Dumbarton, which he founded. The site of Mackinnon's birthplace in Campbeltown, where he started his business career as an apprentice grocer, is marked by a commemorative plaque.

Cottage near Whitehouse

To the north of Clachan the main road climbs up high to moorland, giving extensive views over West Loch Tarbert and the mountains to the north and north-east. Then the road descends, running along the loch, though inland, through the village of Whitehouse, rejoining the shore at the ferry terminal of Kennacraig – just past the road junction for Claonaig and Skipness.

We have now completed the circuit of Kintyre, and explored many of its highways and byways. However, there are many nooks and crannies still to explore – but we leave that to the visitors to discover for themselves. We now take passage for Gigha, to explore a real island!

7 GIGHA

THE ISLAND OF GIGHA (Norse: *gja-ey*, 'cleft island') lies 3 miles (4.8km) west of Kintyre and is reached by ferry from Tayinloan. The journey takes about 20 minutes. The name is pronounced 'gee-ah', with a hard 'g'. The locals prefer to say the name is derived from *Gudey*, meaning 'God's island'. Only 6½ miles long (10.4km) and under 2 miles (3km) wide, it is fertile and productive, supporting a population of about 180, many of whom speak Gaelic. The only village, with the pier, post office and island shop, is Ardminish. The parish church here has a stained glass window commemorating Kenneth Macleod of Eigg, who wrote *The Road to the Isles* and many other songs. The old medieval parish church is at Kilchattan, south of Ardminish; in the burial ground are intricately carved late medieval grave-slabs. Nearby is the 'ogham stone', with an indecipherable inscription in a script brought from Ireland in pre-Christian times.

THE 'BULL OF CRARO'

Following the road past Kilchattan church towards Ardlamey Farm and the cottage named Tigh nan Cudainnean, it is possible to reach the south-west

The ruins of Kilchattan church

Opposite: Stained glass window, parish church, Gigha

shore of Gigha, with safe, sandy beaches ideal for a picnic. Offshore from here is the small island of Craro. The 'Bull of Craro' is a rock formation, only visible from the seaward side, which features in an island story of a local boy who was taken prisoner by pirates off the coast of North Africa. The pirate chief was about to send him to the fate of his colleagues when he heard the boy praying in Gaelic and asked him, in Gaelic, where he was from. When the boy replied that he came from Gigha, the pirate asked him to prove it, by telling him which way the Bull of Craro faced. The boy gave the right answer, and was reprieved.

Further round the coast, at Port a Gharaidh, is a quarry where quernstones, for grinding grain, were made from the epidiorite rock which outcrops all over the island.

ACHAMORE

South of Kilchattan is Achamore House, in private ownership, with surrounding gardens in the care of the National Trust for Scotland since 1962. The gardens and adjoining woodland, with many exotic azalea and rhododendron species, were developed by Sir James Horlick (of bedtime beverage fame) who bought the island in 1944. The whole island, including a fish farm developed in the 1980s, was sold in 1989, amid some controversy and local apprehension.

The Achamore creamery, which produced a fine cheese, is now closed, and the milk produced by the island's dairy herds is transported daily to Campbeltown. The estate, fish farm and small-scale commercial fishing provide a little employment.

ARCHAEOLOGICAL SITES

Despite its small size, there are many archaeological sites on Gigha: cairns, standing stones, forts and duns. There is a fine cairn at the north end (Carn Ban) and an impressive standing stone beside the road overlooking East Tarbert Bay. South-west of Tarbert Farm

Left: Achamore House

Overleaf: East Tarbert Bay

81

Opposite: In the gardens at Achamore House

THE BROWNIE'S CHAIR

Cara is the residence of a family of brownies, those impish and mischievous figures of folklore who amused and occasionally tormented our ancestors.

On landing on the island the visitor must greet the brownies, or risk their annoying interference and possibly some bad luck. The family who lived in the old farmhouse were known to put out a saucer of milk and some food at night to placate the brownies.

Doubters can visit the 'Brownie's Chair', a stone seat on the south-east slopes of Cara, facing Kintyre. This seat is about 39 inches (one metre) square, with a stone back. Don't forget to say goodbye nicely to the brownies when you leave.

are interesting rocky outcrops carved with Early Christian symbols. The finest fort is Dun Chibhich, in the middle of the island, reached (with permission) from Druimyeonbeg Farm. The road to Ardailly, on the west coast of Gigha, passes close to a small Iron Age fort, Dunan an t-Seasgain. Just past Ardailly is another fort, Dun an Trinnse. Two stones near Leim, known as the Bodach and the Cailleach (the old man and the old woman), are likely to be several centuries old, but perhaps not prehistoric.

The island must have been visited by Norse raiders and settlers during their domination of the Hebrides. A Viking grave found by chance in 1849 at East Tarbert Bay produced an ornate portable balance, with decorative pans and weights, now in the Hunterian Museum at the University of Glasgow. It probably belonged to an itinerant Norse metal-worker, dealing in gold and silver, sometime in the eleventh century.

The Norse king Haakon held court in Gigha in 1263, on his way to the Battle of Largs. According to a Norse saga, his court chaplain died on Gigha and was buried at the Cistercian abbey of Saddell on the east side of Kintyre. Until the nineteenth century the island lairds were a branch of the MacNeill clan.

Gigha is an island which takes time to explore properly. In summer the day-trippers come for a few hours and can see a lot in a short time, but it is best to stay on the island for a few days and search out some of the nooks and crannies of the island's history. Unfortunately, some sites are almost inaccessible in summer due to excessive growth of bracken. The view from Creag Bhan, the highest hill 329ft (100m), takes in Kintyre, Knapdale, Islay, Jura, Arran, Rathlin Island and the coastline of Northern Ireland.

This is one island which is best explored by bicycle or on foot. The island's roads are all single track and not really equipped to deal with tourist traffic, especially in the summer months. No part of Gigha is more than 3 miles (4.8km) from the Post Office at Ardminish, and it is often possible to arrange a lift with one of the locals.

There are four piers on Gigha, one at each end of the island and two in the middle. The island is popular with visiting yachts. At one time the ferry from West Loch Tarbert called at Gigha on its way to Islay, but now the new pier at Ardminish is the only one served by Calmac. The pier at the south end is used by some of the island's fishermen.

Off the south end of Gigha are the small islands of Gigalum and Cara. The former farmhouse on Cara has been renovated recently as a holiday house. It is sometimes possible to arrange boat trips to Cara to view the medieval chapel there and the 'Brownie's Chair'.

8 THE LAND AND THE PEOPLE

THE UNDERLYING GEOLOGY OF the landscape of Kintyre is crucial to an understanding of the human geography of the peninsula. Although it lies to the north and west of the Highland Boundary Fault, the gentle rolling farmlands of Kintyre do not immediately suggest a Highland landscape. To emphasise its transitional character, exposures of Old Red Sandstone and Carboniferous rocks are found at the southern end of the Kintyre peninsula. There is much fertile arable land, especially on the loamy soils of the extensive raised beach terraces of the western coastlands, where reduced rainfall also makes for attractive agricultural land – among the best anywhere in Argyll. Metamorphic limestones and Green Beds (taking their name from the mineral chlorite), rich in magnesium and iron, also outcrop along the western coast, bringing fertile soils wherever they occur. This contrasts with the hilly eastern coasts, now largely given over to forests.

In the Laggan, the triangle of low-lying ground between Campbeltown and Machrihanish, Carboniferous Limestone enriches the soil, while around Southend, Old Red Sandstone has a similar effect. The Carboniferous rocks contain great thicknesses of coal measures, matching the Ballycastle coalfield in Ulster, on the other side of the North Channel; there are also calciferous sandstones and contemporary basalts. The existence of these anomalous Carboniferous rocks, completely surrounded by the Dalradian rocks which make up most of Kintyre, is apparently due to fortuitous downfaulting.

Coal was known to exist in Kintyre from at least the fifteenth century, and was mined intermittently from the late seventeenth century until 1967, when the Argyll Colliery was forced to close on economic grounds. A wide range of rocks, minerals and fossils from Kintyre rocks can be seen in the Campbeltown Museum. A visit to this interesting and comprehensive collection of specimens is highly recommended.

Dalradian rocks take their name from the ancient kingdom of Dalriada, whose ruler Kenneth MacAlpin became King of the Picts and Scots in AD843.

Left: Rocks near Skipness

Pages 88–9: The raised beach near Beacharr on the west coast of Kintyre, with the island of Gigha in view

Most of the Kintyre peninsula is made up of quartzose mica schists and schistose grits, although only in the hills around the Mull of Kintyre does the landscape assume the steep and rugged appearance expected after viewing the similarly constituted hills of Knapdale and Cowal. On the eastern side of the peninsula from Crossaig south are mainly chlorite schists, while the west of Kintyre from Tarbert to the Mull of Kintyre is mostly biotite.

The geology of the rocks known as the Dalradian Assemblage is complex. The term is used to include all metamorphosed rocks of late Pre-Cambrian and Lower Palaeozoic age, around 600 million years old, which cover the western mainland of Scotland from the south of Kintyre through Cowal and Knapdale to Lorn, including the eastern part of Islay, and the islands of Jura and Lismore. Different zones have been differentiated according to the degree of pressure and heat which occurred in different areas during the building of the Caledonian mountains, around 400 million years ago. In Kintyre the rocks are of the Upper Dalradian sequence, with intrusive patches of green epidiorite. The north-east/south-west grain of the Kintyre landscape dates from this period.

Dating from about 395 million years ago are the Old Red Sandstone rocks, reddish rocks which make up most of the eastern half of the Mull of Kintyre and the island of Sanda, with small outcrops also on the north side of Campbeltown Loch. The quarry at Dalaruan, which takes its name from the redness of the sandstone, provided much of the building stone for the tenements of Campbeltown. The fine caves at Keil, near the village of Southend, are cut into former sea cliffs of Old Red Sandstone.

Between Machrihanish and Campbeltown are about 12 square miles (19sq km) of Carboniferous deposits, dating from 345–325 million years ago. These contain extensive coal seams, unfortunately no longer worked. It is unusual to find Carboniferous rocks north of the Highland Boundary Fault: the only other examples in Argyll are small pockets at Bridge of Awe, Glas Eilean in the Sound of Islay, and at Inninmore Bay on the north shore of the Sound of Mull.

The cottages along the main road through Drumlemble were built as miners' cottages: the colliery was originally on the north side of the village. Later the pithead was moved nearer Machrihanish, where a caravan park now occupies the site.

The Limestone Coal Group in which the coal seams lie is about 390ft (119m) thick. It contains a number of seams, of which the main coal seam, 10–12ft (3–3.7m) thick, was worked extensively. Plans of the workings in the Public Library in Campbeltown show that they existed on several levels and once extended under the sea. Above the main coal seam was a roof of thick sandstone, also mined underground as a source of moulding sand. About 110ft (33.5m) above this was another worked seam, known as Kilkivan Coal.

Columnar basalt at Macringan's Point, Campbeltown and (below) detail

Above the coal measures is the Upper Limestone Group, up to 290ft (88.3m) thick and containing three to four marine limestones, followed by Millstone Grits consisting of basic lava flows of varying thickness with well-defined boles (clay-like in appearance) of reddish mudstone.

A small area of Permian desert sandstones can be found on the west side of Kintyre, extending for at least eight miles (12.9km) along the coastline. They can be seen between Glenbarr and Bellochantuy, and again north of Glenacardoch Point as far as Killean. These are bright red sandstones with bands of coarse breccia composed of vein-quartz, mica-schist and quartzite. These deposits were at one time assigned to the Upper Old Red Sandstone, but comparisons with the breccia associated with a sea-stack of limestone and schist at Port nan Gallan near the Mull of Oa in Islay, and with the Permian desert sandstone of Mauchline in Ayrshire, have persuaded geologists to revise their earlier opinions. These rocks date from the end of the Palaeozoic era, about 280 million years ago.

Throughout south-west Scotland there are literally hundreds of intrusive igneous tertiary dykes, dating from a period of intense volcanic activity about 60 million years ago, centred mainly in Arran, Mull, Ardnamurchan, and under the sea between Islay and Colonsay. Typically these dykes run north-west or north-north-west, cutting across the north-east/south-west grain of the rocks through which they intrude. The effect is similar to the radiating cracks seen when a stone or bullet passes through a pane of glass. They are best seen on the shoreline: a fine example of a dolerite dyke can be seen at A'Chleit, on the west coast of Kintyre, one mile (1.6km) north of Muasdale. Other fine examples can be seen at Torrisdale, and at Ronachan Point, near Clachan, as well as in dozens of other locations. In some cases the dykes can be traced far inland, running across country, as on the south-west slopes of Beinn an Tuirc.

One of the best sites in Kintyre for geological field study is The Gauldrons, half a mile (0.8km) to the south of the old lifeboat station at Machrihanish. Beds of the calcareous Carboniferous sandstone known as cornstone rest upon a platform of schists. Vertical basalt dykes can be seen in the cliff face, and can be followed across the raised beach and out into the sea. The shingle beach will yield a good range of interesting pebbles, including a few flints, presumably brought there by glacial drift.

Between the Campbeltown Shipyard at Trench Point and the medieval ruins of Kilchousland church, on the north side of Macringan's Point, is a geological curiosity reminiscent of the Giant's Causeway. Columns of basalt about one foot (0.3m) in diameter cover the shore, separated from one another by veins of calc-spar, haematite, and green earthy carbonate of copper. The haematite veins are up to 3–4in (7.6–10cm) wide, though usually less. In a few cases the basalt column has been entirely eroded away, leaving the empty inter-columnar veins, producing a honeycomb effect.

Along with the rest of Argyll, Kintyre was scoured by ice-sheets emanating from the Moor of Rannoch, completely removing any rocks later than

FINDING FOSSILS

There are some interesting fossils in Kintyre. Interspersed among the lavas at Machrihanish are bands of sediments, including a fossiliferous band with remains of gastropods and ribbed brachiopods; examples of fossils can be seen in the Campbeltown Museum, chiefly ferns, roots and the trunks of tree ferns, all evidence of a warm, damp climate. The most unusual is a fossil fish, Gyraconthus formosus.

Pages: 92–3: An Iron Age dun on Dun Skeig Hill, looking up West Loch Tarbert

Kilcolmkill chapel on the raised beach at Southend

the Permian beds already referred to. Flint pebbles found occasionally on Kintyre beaches are intriguing, in view of the fact that in Mesolithic times, from 8000–3500BC, Campbeltown Loch was a major centre of a prehistoric flint-working industry. However, no Cretaceous flint-bearing rocks remain in Kintyre: the nearest source of flint is in Antrim, to the south-west, requiring the pebbles found on Kintyre beaches to have been brought there by ocean currents. Equally, they may have been deposited by glacial drift, in which case their origin would be earlier rocks, now removed by ice action, from north-east Scotland. The sea channels now occupied by Loch Fyne, West Loch Tarbert and Kilbrannan Sound are all the result of glaciation.

There are some excellent examples of raised beaches in Kintyre. There were three or four Ice Ages, with periods of warm climate in between, but after the ice melted, about 25,000 years ago, sea levels rose dramatically. Much of the present coastline of Kintyre would have been flooded to a depth of 25–30ft (7.6–9.1m), so the Mull of Kintyre would have been separated from the rest of the peninsula at the Laggan, and Kintyre would have been an island, cut off from the mainland at what is now the isthmus of Tarbert. The flat ground inland from Rhunahaorine Point at Tayinloan would have been inundated, as well as some of the river valleys.

However, by 6,000BC the sea had dropped to almost its present level as the land recovered from the tremendous weight of thousands of feet of ice. The beaches and cliffs which had been created when the sea level was higher were now left high and dry, and form some of the most spectacular geological scenery in Kintyre. Most of the west coast road from Tarbert to Campbeltown is on the raised beach, and it is seen particularly well around the edges of the Laggan and at Campbeltown Loch, especially on the south side between Kilkerran and Kildalloig. Associated storm beaches, now often far removed from the present shoreline, can also be seen. A fine example of successive storm beaches can be seen at Saddell Bay.

Alluvial deposits create some of the most fertile land in Kintyre, apart from the limestone levels already mentioned. Outstanding among the areas of marine alluvia is the Laggan, between Machrihanish and Campbeltown, now that it has been drained and cleared almost entirely of peat growth. The same could be said of the coast north and south of Tayinloan. There are several fertile areas covered with freshwater alluvia, of which the best are the valley of the Lussa River, flowing into Kilbrannan Sound at Peninver, Saddell Glen, Torrisdale Glen, Carrade and Rhonadale, while on the west coast there is good ground in the valleys inland from Clachan and Glenbarr. At the south end of Kintyre, Glen Breackerie and Conie Glen are both very fertile.

Apart from coal, now no longer worked, there are no mineral resources in Kintyre which could be exploited on a large scale. There is a small limestone quarry at Calliburn which provides ground limestone for farmers and gravel for road-making material. There are sand and gravel

Beautiful blue skies over the yachting pontoon in Campbeltown harbour

pits at Dhurrie, near the airport, and at Langa Farm, near Kilchenzie, providing sand and different grades of gravel for building contractors.

Opposite: *Unloading prawns at West Loch Pier, Tarbert*

Pages 98–9: *To the east of Tarbert, this beach is made of scallop shells*

CLIMATE

The climate of Kintyre is very favourable for agriculture, despite the impression of incessant wind and rain. The glens of Kintyre are generally sheltered and fertile. In the *Old Statistical Account* for Saddell and Skipness, the local minister wrote in 1792 that: 'During the summer and autumn, the degree of heat in these glens is very great, but they are frequently refreshed with drizzling rains and flying showers.' Usually the best land in the Kintyre glens is where they meet the sea, with often a flat, alluvial 'delta' of extremely fertile ground jutting out into the sea. In the eighteenth century the farm houses were often built so as to have the best land between them and the shore. Further inland were the 'outfields' used for oats and pasture. These lands were 'subdivided into small enclosures with earthen fences, formerly used as folds for their cattle'. In some glens, traces of this early landscape survive.

Visitors will quickly learn that in Kintyre the weather can change suddenly. In the *Old Statistical Account* it was noted that 'the transitions from mild to cold, from dry to wet, are sudden and frequent, embarrassing the projects, and disappointing the expectations, of the husbandman'. And, we could add, of modern tourists.

As we have already seen, the first decision the wheeled explorer has to make after entering Kintyre is whether to zoom down the west coast road to Campbeltown, or to cross over to the east side and proceed at a more leisurely pace on a narrower, twistier road. Writing in 1792, the Rev Mr George Macliesh advanced the cause of the east coast road, which he thought to be

... preferable in many respects. It is equally short, and much more pleasant, from the great variety of beautiful objects which present themselves successively to travellers, as they journey either along a delightful bank within view of the sea, or are suddenly sunk into pleasant woods and valleys, where every sense is entertained, and the mind is relieved from that disgusting sameness, which in open extended plains, fatigues the traveller more than the length of the road.

The same minister noted the amount of work required to ensure adequate fuel for a family:

Turf or peats were their only fuel: they are found in the hills; but the cutting, with the whole expensive process of drying and carrying them home, used to occupy the farmer and his whole family for a great part of the summer season, and in a wet season, he ran the dreadful risk of wanting [lacking] fire to dress his victuals, or warm him during the inclemency of winter.

Useful Information and Places to Visit

Tourist Information Centre, Campbeltown
MacKinnon House, The Pier, Campbeltown,
Argyll PA28 6EF
Tel: 01586 552056
Fax: 01586 553291
Accommodation bookings, leaflets, books, maps.
Information on bus services, taxis, car hire, services,
events, festivals, yacht charters, etc. Open all year.

Tourist Information Centre, Tarbert
Harbour Street, Tarbert, Argyll PA29 6UD
Tel: 01880 820429
Fax: 01880 820082
Accommodation bookings, leaflets, books, maps.
Information on local facilities. Open April to October.

Local newspaper
Campbeltown Courier
Main Street & Longrow South, Campbeltown,
Argyll PA28 6AE
Tel: 01586 554646
Fax: 01586 553006
Published weekly on Friday.

Travel

Caledonian MacBrayne, Kennacraig
Ferry Terminal, Kennacraig, Whitehouse,
By Tarbert, Argyll PA29 6YF
Tel: 01880 730253
Fax: 01880 730202
Brochure hotline: 01475 650288
Information on ferry services to Islay, Gigha, Arran
(Lochranza) and Cowal (Portavadie).

Argyll and Antrim Steam Packet Company
The Ferry Terminal, Hall Street, Campbeltown,
Argyll PA28 6BU
Tel: 0990 523523 for reservations and information.
Ferry services from Campbeltown to Ballycastle, May
to October.

Stained glass in the parish church, Gigha

*Opposite: Maggie's Cottage viewed from the old byre at
An Tairbeart Heritage Centre*

Paddle Steamer Waverley
Waverley Excursions Ltd,
Anderston Quay, Glasgow G3 8HA
Tel: 0141 221 8152   Fax: 0141 248 2150
Information on excursions to Campbeltown and the Mull
of Kintyre also available from the TIC in Campbeltown.

Loganair
Campbeltown Airport, Campbeltown, Argyll PA28 6NU
Tel: 0345 222111 (reservations)
Tel: 01586 553873 (information)
Fax: 01586 552571
Daily flights to/from Glasgow Airport.

THINGS TO DO

Argyll Bowling Club
Millknowe, Campbeltown, Argyll PA28 6NG
Tel: 01586 554676

Campbeltown Bowling Club
Stronvaar, New Quay Street, Campbeltown, Argyll
Tel: 01586 553193

Campbeltown Swimming Pool
Kinloch Road, Campbeltown, Argyll PA28 6EG
Tel: 01586 553037

Dunaverty Golf Club
Southend, Argyll PA28 6RW
Tel: 01586 830677

Forest Enterprise
Whitegates, Lochgilphead, Argyll PA31 8RS
Tel: 01546 602518
Forest walks at Carradale and Beinn Ghuilean,
Campbeltown.

Machrihanish Golf Club
Machrihanish, Campbeltown, Argyll PA28 6PT
Tel: 01586 810213
Fax: 01586 810221
Tee reservations: 01586 810277

Port Righ from the golf course at Carradale

Tarbert Golf Club
Kilberry Road, Tarbert, Argyll
Tel: 01880 820565

PLACES TO VISIT

An Tairbeart Heritage Centre
Tarbert, Argyll PA29 6SX
Tel: 01880 820190
Fax: 01880 820102
Open 10am till sunset, 7 days a week, all year round.
Admission charged to exhibition areas.

Campbeltown Heritage Centre
The Vestry, Lorne Street Church, The Big Kiln,
Campbeltown, Argyll
Tel: 01586 551400
Open Easter to September, Monday to Friday, 12noon
to 5pm; Saturday, 10am to 5pm; Sunday, 2pm to 5pm.
Admission charged.

Campbeltown Picture House
26 Hall Street, Campbeltown, Argyll
Tel: 01586 553657; after 7pm, 01586 553899

Campbeltown Public Library and Museum
Hall Street, Campbeltown, Argyll
Tel: 01586 552366 and 01586 552367

Carradale Network Centre
Carradale, Argyll
Tel/Fax: 01583 431296
Open May to October, 10.30am to 4.30pm; Sunday,
12noon to 4pm. Admission charged.

Earra Gael
The Weighbridge, Tarbert, Argyll PA29 6UD
Tel: 01880 820428

Oyster farm at Clachan

Open April to October, including Sundays in high season. Showpiece craft shop for Argyll craft workers.

Glenbarr Abbey
Macalister Clan Visitor Centre, Glenbarr,
By Tarbert, Argyll PA29 6UT
Tel: 01583 421247
Fax: 01583 421255
Open daily except Tuesday, April to October.
Admission charged.

Grogport Tannery
The Old Manse, Grogport, Carradale,
Argyll PA28 6QL
Tel: 01583 431255
Open daily, 9am to 6pm.

Springbank Distillery
J. and A. Mitchell Co. Ltd, Well Close, Longrow,
Campbeltown, Argyll PA28 6ET
Tel: 01586 552085
Fax: 01586 553215
Guided tours by prior arrangement only.

PLACE-NAMES AND THEIR MEANINGS

These are just a few of the hundreds of place-names in Kintyre and Gigha, most of them derived from Gaelic (G) or Norse (N) words – sometimes in combination.

Ardnacross	G. *ard na croise*	the point of the cross
Auchincorvey	G. *achadh na-cairbhe*	field of the carcass
Amod	N. *a-mot*	river meeting
Ballivain	G. *bail'a'mheadhoin*	middle-township
Baraskomil	G. *barr* + N. *askr*	ash tree headland
Beachmore	G. *beitheach mhor*	the big birchwood
Bealochgair	G. *bealach-gearr*	the short pass
Beinn an Tuirc	G. *beinn an tuirc*	mountain of the wild boar
Borgadale	N. *borg-dalr*	fort glen
Breakachy	G. *breac-achadh*	the speckled field
Carradale	N. *kjarr-dalr*	brush-wood valley
Cattadale	N. *kottr-dalr*	cat valley
Chiscan	G. *sescenn*	boggy land
Clochkeil	G. *clach gheal*	white stone
Cnoc Scalbert	G. *cnoc*; N. *skallis-bolstadr*	hill of Skalli's (nicknamed 'Baldy') farm
Crossaig	N. *kross-vik*	cross bay
Dalivaddy	G. *dail a'mhadaidh*	place of the wolf
Davaar	G. *da bharr*	two headlands
Deucheran	G. *diubh cheathramhnan*	the two quarterlands
Dirigadal	N. *dyr-dalr*	deer valley
Dorlinn	G. *doirlinn*	tidal strip of land, isthmus
Drumlemble	G. *druim leamhan*	ridge of the elms
Dunaverty	G. *dun a'bhardainn*	the fort of the warning
Feorlan	G. *feoirling*	farthing land
Gigha	N. *gja-ey*	rift island
Glecknahavil	G. *glac an t-sabhail*	the small valley of the barn
Glenahanty	G. *gleann-shean-tighe*	the glen of the old house
Glenramskill	G. *gleann*; N. *ranis-gil*	the glen of the hog-backed ridge ravine
Guesdale	N. *gas-dalr*	goose valley
Ifferdale	N. *yfir-dalr*	the upper valley
Kilblaan	G. *cill-Bhlathain*	the church of St Blaan
Kilchrist	G. *cill-Chriosd*	the church of Christ
Kilchattan	G. *cill-Chatain*	St Catan's church
Kilchenzie	G. *cill-Choinnich*	St Kenneth's church
Kilchousland	G. *cill-Chuisilein*	St Constantine's church
Kileonain	G. *cill-Adhamhnain*	Adamnan's church

Kilkerran	G. *cill-Chiarain*	St Ciaran's church
Kilkivan	G. *cill-Chaomhain*	St Coivin's church
Killean	G. *cill-ghille-Iain*	church of the servants of St John
Killocraw	G. *coille chno*	nut wood
Kilmichael	G. *cill-Mhicheil*	St Michael's church
Kintyre	G. *Cinn-tire*	the head of the land, 'Land's End'
Kirnashie	G. *coire na sith*	the corrie of peace, the fairy dell
Lussa	N. *ljoss*	bright, clear, shining river
Machrihanish	G. *machair sean-innse*	the plain of the old haugh
Muasdale	N. *munkr-dalr*	monk's valley
Ormsary	N. *Ormr* + G. *airidh*	Orm's (nicknamed 'Snake') shieling
Peninver	G. *peighinn an inbhir*	the Inver pennyland
Putechantuy	G. *put-achan-an t-suidhe*	the sitting place of the moorfowl
Ranachan	G. *raineachan*	bracken
Rhonadale	N. *reynir-dalr*	rowan-tree valley
Ronachan	G. *ron achan*	the place of seals
Rhunahaorine	G. and N. *rudha na eyrr ine*	the gravelly point
Ru Staffnish	G. *rudha*; N. *stafr-nes*	column-point promontory
Saddell	N. *sandr-dalr*	sandy valley
Skipness	N. *skip-nes*	ship point
Smerby	N. *smjorr-bolstadr*	butter farm
Sunadale	N. *sunne-dalr*	south valley
Tangy	N. *tangi*	a tongue of land
Tayinloan	G. *tigh an loin*	the marsh house
Tirfergus	G. *tir-Fergus*	Fergus's land
Torrisdale	N. *Thors-dalr*	Thor's valley
Ugadale	N. *ugla-dalr*	owl valley

FURTHER READING

Campbeltown Public Library has an excellent local history collection, and holds files of the local newspaper, the *Campbeltown Courier*. The Library of the Kintyre Antiquarian and Natural History Society has some rare pamphlet material and some unpublished manuscripts. Their *Magazine* is an excellent source of information on Kintyre. A bibliography of published books and articles on Kintyre would take many pages, but the following items are good introductions to the area and should be fairly easy to obtain through libraries. The books by Angus Martin, including his works of poetry, give unrivalled insight into the social history and contemporary 'feel' of Kintyre.

Carmichael, Alastair *Kintyre: Best of all the Isles* (David & Charles, 1974)

McKerral, Andrew *Kintyre in the Seventeenth Century* (Oliver & Boyd, 1948)

MacMillan, Nigel *The Campbeltown & Machrihanish Light Railway* (David & Charles, 1970)

Martin, Angus *The Ring-net Fishermen* (John Donald, 1981)

Martin, Angus *Kintyre: The Hidden Past* (John Donald, 1984)

Martin, Angus *Kintyre Country Life* (John Donald, 1987)

Martin, Angus *The Larch Plantation* (Macdonald Publishers, 1990)

Martin, Angus *The Song of the Quern* (Scottish Cultural Press, 1998)

Martin, Angus *Tales of Kintyre Fishermen* (Tuckwell Press, 1998)

Royal Commission on the Ancient and Historical Monuments of Scotland *Argyll: An Inventory of the Ancient Monuments. Vol. 1, Kintyre.* (1971)

INDEX

Page numbers in *italic* indicate illustrations